Exodus:
Lessons In Freedom

*How To Get Free,
Stay Free And
Set Others Free*

Eric Elder

Exodus: Lessons In Freedom
Copyright © 2005-2007 Eric Elder.
All rights reserved.

Exodus: Lessons In Freedom is part of a series of inspirational resources produced by Eric Elder Ministries. For a boost in your faith anytime, please visit:
WWW.THERANCH.ORG

Cover image provided by Michael Swanson.
http://blogs.msdn.com/mswanson/
articles/wallpaper.aspx

All scripture quotations are taken from The Holy Bible, New International Version. Copyright © 1973, 1978, 1984 by International Bible Society. Used by permission of Zondervan Publishing House. All rights reserved.

ISBN 978-1-931760-24-9

DEDICATION

To the Lord, Jesus Christ—
for setting me free.

Acknowledgments

Special thanks to the following people for their help and encouragement during the creation of this study:

Lana Elder, Jim Allen, Jim and Holly Bressner, Alan and Laurie Brewer, Rob Dickman, Bud Gautschy, Dee Gaylord, Al Lowry, Ralph McClure, Eric Negray, James Olmos, Scott and Lisa Palm, Jessica Pastirik, Greg Potzer, Dale, Judy and Tyson Ralston, Butch Ringwald, Sue Roberts, Dale Ruff, Paul, Penny and Paul M.Seipp, Rich Schmidt, Kurt Smith, Mark Upchurch, Jamie Vitton and the pastors of the Streator Ministerial Association.

Preface

Exodus is one of the most dramatic, yet practical books in the Bible. Feature films have told various stories from the book of Exodus, ranging from Cecil B. Demille's epic, *The Ten Commandments,* to DreamWorks' animated, *The Prince of Egypt,* to Stephen Spielberg's classic, *Raiders of the Lost Ark.*

But what I like most about the book of Exodus is not how dramatic it is, but how practical it is.

I began this study at a time when I wanted to expand my own ministry. I wanted to learn how God used Moses to set hundreds of thousands of people free. I thought I might learn a few lessons for how God might use me to set others free, too.

I was right. But instead of finding one or two lessons, I found fifty!

I began applying these lessons to my own life and ministry and began to see results immediately. These are the lessons that I'll be sharing with you throughout this book—lessons from stories that are over 3,000 years old, and lessons from from my own life today; lessons that include some of my favorite Bible stories, and lessons that include some of my favorite personal stories of my own walk with God.

God wants to set you free. He wants to keep you free. And He wants to use you to set others free. May God bless you—and many others—as you read and apply these lessons to your life.

Eric Elder

P.S. I've included a Scripture Reading with each devotional that I encourage you to read in your own Bible as well as reading my devotional. It's a great way to hear directly from God about subjects in your life that I may not have touched upon in my devotional, and when you've read all of the Scripture Readings, you'll have also read through the entire book of Exodus.

Lesson 1

THE FEAR OF MAN LEADS TO BONDAGE

Scripture Reading: Exodus 1:1-14

Could it be that your greatest weakness is actually your greatest strength?

A man came up to me after I spoke at a men's breakfast and said, "Hi Eric, do you remember me?" I strained to put a name with his face, but couldn't do it. When he told me his name, an image from high school immediately flashed across my mind.

We were both freshmen playing flag football in gym class when he got in the way of a senior. This senior knocked my friend to the ground and started pummeling him in the face with his fist. I watched my friend's head bounce up and down on the ground with each pounding.

Why would someone pummel my friend like that? My friend was a big kid, but a nice kid. Even though he hadn't done anything wrong, his sheer size made him appear to be a threat. The pummeling had its effect: my friend never got in this senior's way again, and I made sure I didn't either!

Unfortunately, my friend walked away feeling weak and beaten down when in reality, it was his sheer strength that drew the fire in the first place. When people are fearful of us, or we're fearful of them, it often leads to bondage. Something similar happened to the Israelites. Back in the days of Moses, when the nation of Israel started to grow while they were living in Egypt, the king of Egypt saw their strength and got scared:

> *"Look," he said to his people, "the Israelites have become much too numerous for us. Come, we must deal shrewdly with them or they will become even more numerous and, if war breaks out, will join our enemies, fight against us and leave the country" (Exodus 1:9-10).*

The Israelites were immediately enslaved. For the next 400 years, they were treated as the lowest of the low in Egypt. I'm sure they felt worthless, worn-out and weak. But in reality, it was their great strength that caused the fearful king to put them into bondage. Although they may have felt like the weakest nation on earth, do you remember what God said about them? He called them His "chosen" people, His "treasured possession," and promised that they would become "a great nation." (Deuteronomy 7:6 and Genesis 12:2). This was their destiny. This was their calling. A destiny and calling that the king foresaw and tried to stop.

I got spiritually pummeled a few years ago after speaking as a guest at a local church. I thought the regular pastor would be thrilled when he came back to hear that half a dozen people had put their faith in Christ that day for the very first time. Instead, I got an extremely harsh letter from him a few weeks later saying that one of those people had started going to another church (she wanted to go to a Bible study and her church didn't have one). He blamed me for her leaving and made it clear that he wanted nothing to do with me or my ministry ever again.

For the next few days, I felt like I'd gotten the wind knocked out of me. I felt like I never wanted to speak at another church again. This man was not only an influential pastor in the community, but he was also the president of the minister's association in town. But then God reminded me of my calling, my purpose in life, and what *He* said about me. I was able to shake off the fear of man and stand tall again in the calling of God. That pastor eventually invited me to speak again at his church, and I eventually became president of the minister's association! :)

But the fear of man almost derailed me from God's plan for my life. I began to look at other areas of my life where I felt weak to see if those areas might really be strengths instead.

Do you feel weak, pummeled or beaten down in certain areas of your life? Could it be that some of those areas might actually be some of your greatest strengths?

Don't let the fear of man keep you down. Ask God what *He* says about you, your gifts and your calling. Listen to what He says and He will set you free.

Lesson 2

The Fear Of God Leads To Freedom

Scripture Reading: Exodus 1:15-22

I love playing the piano, but I used to be so afraid of playing in front of others that I never wanted to play in public. At home, I could play for hours, loving every minute of it. But in front of others, my brain would check out, and my hands would shake.

Then one day I was reading Jesus' parable about the talents and the three guys who were given different amounts of talents. Two of them made a return on their gifts, but one buried his talent in the ground because he was afraid.

I was convicted. I was letting the "fear of man" keep my talent hidden, when God had given it to me, not just for me but, like all gifts He gives, so that we can bless others.

I had a choice to make: I was going to be guided either by what men might think of me, or by what God might think of me.

The Hebrew midwives in Egypt had a

choice to make, too. When the king of Egypt was afraid the Israelites were growing too numerous and might one day leave them, he put them in bondage and ordered the midwives to kill any baby boys as soon as they were born. What could the midwives do? Their hands were tied—or were they? The Bible says:

"The midwives, however, feared God and did not do what the king of Egypt had told them to do; they let the boys live." (Exodus 1:17)

And the results?

"So God was kind to the midwives and the people increased and became even more numerous. And because the midwives feared God, he gave them families of their own" (Exodus 1:20-21).

Although the "fear of man" threatened to keep the midwives in bondage, the "fear of God" set them free. God honored the midwives' healthy fear of Him by blessing them with families of their own and freeing who-knows-how-many children from the grip of death as well.

Instead of succumbing to their honest and

understandable fears, God showed them a way around their fears to accomplish what He called them to do: deliver His children.

I found a way around my fear of playing the piano in front of people, too.

One day a friend came to my house and heard a few of the songs I had written. He seemed to be truly touched by the music and thought it would touch others, too. He was a professional musician and asked if he could bring some recording equipment over and record the songs. That was fine with me. I wasn't afraid of making a mistake in front of a machine—just people!

When we finished recording a dozen songs, he gave me a copy of the music. I was amazed by what I heard! I had never heard my songs played before as a "listener." I was always the "player," and my concentration was intensely focused on getting the notes right. For the first time, I was able to truly relax and just listen to the music. And it touched my own heart, too.

I uploaded the songs on the Internet and people began to listen. And they were touched, too, setting them free from worries, tensions, fears and doubts that were keeping them in bondage.

Instead of succumbing to my honest and understandable fears, God showed me a way around my fears to accomplish what He called me to do: deliver His children. And the confidence that has given me has enabled me to play in front of people now, too, not caring so much about the notes I might get wrong, but caring more about the notes God's given me to play.

Is the "fear of man" holding you back from doing some of the very things that God has called you to do, gifted you to do, and equipped you to do? You might want to take a cue from the Hebrew midwives who feared God more than man, and in the process set themselves—and who knows how many others—free.

Lesson 3

A Burning Heart Precedes A Burning Bush

Scripture Reading: Exodus 2

Do you ever wish God would just show up in a burning bush and tell you clearly what He wanted you to do?

Then I have some good news for you: I believe God wants to do that for you, too! Why? Because while we're looking for a burning bush, God is looking for a burning heart—one that burns with the same desires for which His burns.

When I take a close look at the years leading up to Moses' burning bush experience, I can't help but think that God didn't choose Moses at random. In chapter 2 of Exodus, we read that Moses' heart was bent on rescuing people years before God called him to rescue an entire nation. Three times in the passage preceding the burning bush, we see a burning heart:

1) He tries to rescue a fellow Hebrew who was being beaten by an Egyptian;
2) He tries to rescue two fighting Hebrews from each other;
3) He tries to rescue Jethro's daughters from the attacking shepherds.

Here's a man whose heart was set on rescuing people. So when God was looking for a man to rescue the entire nation of Israel from slavery, to whom did He look? To Moses, a man whose heart was already burning to do the very things that God wanted done.

The lesson for me in this passage is that a burning heart precedes a burning bush. Sometimes we're looking for a burning bush when God is looking for a burning heart. He's looking to see if we're eager to do the things that He wants done. And when He sees a burning heart, He often puts His finger on that person and says, "I choose you for this task because you have shown yourself eager to do the very things I want done."

I remember hearing a pastor from Germany speak to a group of us in the United States, asking if any of us wanted to join him in doing missionary work in Germany. Several hands went up. Then he asked, "Okay, what things have you been doing here in the U.S. with Germanic people?" None of those in the audience had an answer for him. He continued, "When I see that you're working with Germanic people here and that you truly have a heart for them, then let's talk about coming over to Germany and helping me with my work. I want to know that your heart is really in it."

I had some friends who had a heart for Chinese people. They wanted to go to China someday to live and laugh and learn and share with the Chinese. So they started by inviting Chinese people into their home while they lived in the United States. They did this for several years. When God was looking for someone to go to China, whom do you think God called? They eventually moved to China to live among their people God had put on their heart, and were able to change even more lives for Him.

When you look at the lives of people like Moses, the Apostle Paul and Joseph, you'll see that while each of them had rather dramatic "burning bush" experiences, their ultimate calling was not radically different from what they had been doing all along: serving God with their whole hearts and doing His will all along the way.

There's good news in all of this for you, too: know that while you're looking for a burning bush, God is looking for a burning heart. In fact, He's actively looking throughout the earth for people whose hearts are fully committed to Him. 2 Chronicles 16:9a says:

"For the eyes of the LORD range throughout the earth to strengthen those whose hearts are fully committed to him."

God is continually looking at our hearts. Are they fully committed to Him? Are they burning to do the things that He wants done?

If so, know that God wants to strengthen you in the work you're doing. If not, pray that God will set your heart on fire today for the things that fire Him up. Either way, be encouraged! Once your heart is burning for God, He'll see it, and He may even speak to you in your own "burning bush."

Lesson 4

GOD RESCUES PEOPLE THROUGH PEOPLE

Scripture Reading: Exodus 3:1-10

Ever wonder why, when God wants something done, He calls on one of us to do it instead of just doing it Himself?

I knew a man who was burdened by the problem of pornography in our country and cried out to God: "Don't You see what's happening? How long are You going to let this go on? When are You going to do something about it?"

Then he heard God speaking those same words right back to him: "Don't you see what's happening? How long are you going to let this go on? When are you going to do something about it?"

The man was so convicted that he started an organization to combat the problem, served on a presidential task force to deal with it, and worked for years to try to set people free from this particular bondage.

As I read about Moses and the burning bush in Exodus, chapter 3, I put myself in Moses' shoes for a minute (except that he had taken his off, of course, as God had told him that he was standing on "holy ground"). If I were Moses, I think I would have been fine with everything God was saying up until the last line. Sentence after sentence, God talked about everything He wanted to do for the Israelites, then the conversation took a sharp turn:

"I am the God of your fathers..."
"I have seen the misery of my people..."
"I have heard them crying out..."
"I am concerned about their suffering..."
"I have come down to rescue them..."
"So now go. I am sending you...to bring my people...out of Egypt"

What?!?! I was with You God up until that last line! If *You're* God, if *You* see their misery, if *You've* heard them crying out, if *You're* concerned about their suffering, if *You've* come down to rescue them, then why don't *You* do it! *You* could do this way better than I could!

God Rescues People Through People

No doubt, God was certainly involved. There's no way Moses could have caused the plagues, split the Red Sea, or made the Egyptians gladly give the Israelites all their gold and jewels on their way out of town. But for some reason, God called on Moses to be involved. He told Moses what He was planning to do, then invited Moses to "jump into the story." It's scary, but exciting, that God would let us take part in what He's trying to do on the earth.

The lesson I get out of this is that God likes to rescue people through people. He wants us to be His hands, His feet, His eyes, His ears, His mouth.

A few friends asked me to come pray for a man who was dying of cancer. He was way too young to be on his death bed, and he let me know it. He had a lot of questions for God, saying, "God, what are You doing?" "Why are You doing this to me?" and "Where are You, God?"

I understood what He was saying, but I said, "If you want to know where God is, look around this room! You've got five people standing here by your bedside, praying for you, holding your hand, and talking to you.

He's all around your bed! God lives in us and works through each one of us by His Holy Spirit."

Maybe you're reading these words today and thinking, "That's nice for that guy in his bed, but there's no one talking to me. Where is God for me?" Well, I'm talking to you right now! As you read these words, I hope you'll be able to hear the voice of God in them for you, too, because He wants to tell you something, too: "I love you, I care about you, and you know what? I want to use you, too!"

Why does God use people to rescue people? The Apostle Paul says it this way:

"We are therefore Christ's ambassadors, as though God were making his appeal through us. We implore you on Christ's behalf: Be reconciled to God." (2 Corinthians 5:20).

Let God use you to do His will today.

Lesson 5

LET GOD'S WILL OVERCOME YOUR WON'T

Scripture Reading: Exodus 3:11-4:31

Have you ever faced a choice between God's "will" and your "won't"? A few years ago I felt God wanted me to go to Israel. I had just quit my job and had about $1,500 in the bank. It wasn't exactly the best time to take a trip! But I couldn't get it off my mind, so I called to find out how much a ticket would be. The answer: $1,498!

Two thoughts went through my head simultaneously, one was mine and one was God's. I said, "God, I don't have enough!" while God said, "Eric, you have just enough!" I knew I had a decision to make. Was I going to follow God's "will," or follow my "won't"?

When God calls us to do something that we're afraid to do, how can we overcome our doubts and fears so they don't get in the way of God's will? God gives us a clue in the story of Moses at the burning bush in Exodus, chapters 3 and 4.

When God spoke to Moses from within the burning bush, it was an experience most of us would envy, hearing God speak exactly what to do, personally and clearly. God said: "So now go, I am sending you to Pharaoh to bring my people the Israelites out of Egypt."

But Moses protested. He had already tried to rescue just a few Israelites and that didn't seem to go too well. So Moses said to God, "Who am I, that I should go to Pharaoh and bring the Israelites out of Egypt?"

He had a good question, one we often ask ourselves when God calls us to do something: "Who am I?"

But God had a good answer, the same answer He often gives to us, an answer that contains some of the most comforting words in the whole Bible: "I will be with you." It's worth repeating over and over. "I will be with you." "I will be with you." "I will be with you."

Knowing that God will be with you can help you submit your won't to God's will. Maybe you've heard these classic lines by an unknown author, but they're worth repeating over and over, too:

A basketball in my hands is worth about $19.
A basketball in Michael Jordan's hands is worth about $33 million.
It depends on whose hands it's in.

A sling shot in my hands is a kid's toy.
A sling shot in David's hand is a mighty weapon.
It depends on whose hands it's in.

Two fish and 5 loaves of bread in my hands is a couple of fish sandwiches.
Two fish and 5 loaves of bread in Jesus' hands will feed thousands.
It depends on whose hands it's in.

Nails in my hands might produce a birdhouse.
Nails in Jesus Christ's hands will produce salvation for the entire world.
It depends on whose hands it's in.

As you see now, it depends on whose hands it's in. So put your concerns, your worries, your fears, your hopes, your dreams, your families, and your relationships in God's hands, because, *"It depends on whose hands it's in."*

When Moses was convinced that God would be with him, he finally submitted his won't to God's will. God went with Moses to Egypt and together they set the Israelites free. When I was convinced that God would be with me, I finally submitted my won't to God's will, too. God went with me to Israel and we were both tremendously blessed.

God called my wife, our two oldest kids and me to go on a missions trip to Africa. I looked at the cost and said, "God, I can't do it!" To which God seemed to reply, "It's not a matter of whether you can or can't do it, but whether you will or won't do it. Remember, I will be with you and you can do all things through Christ who gives you strength." So we put a deposit down on the trip and prayed for God's will to be done. It was!

Don't let your won't stand in the way of God's will. Remember, God says, "I will be with you."

Lesson 6

THE BATTLE OF FAITH AND FLESH

Scripture Reading: Exodus 5

What happens when you step out in faith, thinking you're doing what God wants you to do, but then everything goes wrong?

Don't give up on God too soon! You might find that you're still in the center of God's will—even when everything around you looks worse than ever before.

This happens all the time in the "natural" world. Last summer we hired some guys to fix the broken brick steps that lead up to our house. Within a few days we had a bigger mess than before! The yard was piled with broken bricks and concrete, mounds of sand, bags of cement and stacks of new bricks, not to mention the torn up grass from the backhoe and cement truck. It was a total mess, worse than the one we were trying to fix!

The same thing happened to Moses in Exodus 5, with much more devastating results.

He did exactly what God told him to do, asking Pharaoh to let the Israelites go out into the desert for a worship service. The Israelites were thrilled! God had sent a deliverer. But instead of things getting better, things got worse—much worse!

Pharaoh said, "No way!" and ordered the Israelite slaves to continue making the same number of bricks as before, but he'd no longer give them any straw to make the bricks —they would have to find it themselves. The slaves took a beating and they took it out on Moses: "May the Lord look upon you and judge you! You have made us a stench to Pharaoh and his officials and have put a sword in their hand to kill us."

Now Moses faced a battle on two fronts: a battle of faith and a battle of flesh. Although he probably wanted to fight the battle of the flesh first, saving his people from the physical attack coming against them, he knew which battle he had to fight first. He had to fight for his faith—to keep on believing what God had told him. Had he heard from God or not? Had he done something wrong or not? He knew he had to win the battle for his faith first if he was ever going to win the battle of the flesh.

So he did the best thing any of us can do: he returned to the Lord.

He cried out, "O Lord, why have you brought trouble upon this people? Is this why you sent me? Ever since I went to Pharaoh to speak in your name, he has brought trouble upon this people, and you have not rescued your people at all." God answered him, telling him he was right on track and to keep moving forward in faith.

While we were in the middle of our own brick project, I faced another situation that was so frustrating that I wrote in my journal, "I'm pulling my hair out! I want to scream!" I was trying to redesign *The Ranch* website so I could expand it to minister to more people over the Internet. That meant I had to install some new software that I felt God wanted me to use, but I had no idea how to use it. Everything I tried made a bigger mess than before. Instead of making things better, I was making them worse—much worse!

I went outside and looked at the mess in our front yard. I knew that remodeling projects were always like this. When in the middle of it, the mess gets worse before it gets better. I thanked God for the reminder and went back to work.

The website ended up more beautiful and more functional than I could have imagined. Our front steps turned out better than before and the grass began to grow again. These were small victories compared to what Moses finally gained: he was able to set an entire nation free as God had promised.

Just because your steps of faith lead you into worse trouble than before, don't automatically assume that you're out of God's will, or that you've done something wrong. Return to the Lord. Fight the battle of faith first, and the victory in the flesh will follow.

Lesson 7

God Helps Us With Both Battles

Scripture Reading: Exodus 6

How well do you do on the "Wednesdays" of your life? The way you handle those "hump days" could very well determine what happens with the rest of your week—and the rest of your life!

Maybe it's a marriage that you were really thrilled about jumping into at first, but then starts getting hard. Or maybe it's a baby you've looked forward to having and then it finally comes—along with the dirty diapers, the crying and the sleepless nights. Or maybe it's a Bible study you couldn't wait to start, but then begins to lag and just isn't "speaking to you" anymore. Whatever it is, a "Wednesday" is anything that makes you feel like you just want to throw in the towel and give in.

Moses was definitely having a "Wednesday" in Exodus chapter 6, and the lesson God gave him for how to get through it is a good one for us, too.

Moses had done exactly what God told him to do, asking Pharaoh to "Let my people go." But Pharaoh said, "No," and increased the people's work.

Now Moses was fighting a battle in his flesh *and* a battle in his faith. We find out, in Exodus chapter 6, when Moses returns to the Lord, that God is still with him, ready and willing to help Moses fight both battles. Regarding the battle of the flesh, God says He will help Moses by using His "mighty hand":

"Then the LORD said to Moses, 'Now you will see what I will do to Pharaoh: Because of my mighty hand he will let them go; because of my mighty hand he will drive them out of his country' " (Exodus 6:1)

Regarding the battle of the faith, God tells Moses three things:
1) God reminds Moses that this was His idea, His plan, His covenant (verses 2-5);
2) God reminds Moses that He will be with Moses, that Moses isn't fighting alone (verse 6);
3) God reminds Moses what the outcome

will be, what the future holds (verses 7-8).

When you're in the middle of your own battles, be sure to return to the Lord. Let Him speak to you, remind you, reassure you that you're on the right path. If you're not, He'll let you know. But if you are, let Him reassure you that that this is His idea, that He is with you and that He has a plan for your future. These reminders can give you the faith you need to make another push in your flesh, to go another round, to keep moving forward till "Friday" comes.

I had a dream one night where God spoke clearly to me about preaching on the Internet. Even though I thought it would be financially impossible, I saw in the dream an envelope wrapped in a "net"—something that looked like one of those red woven sacks in which they sell grapefruit. There were a few dollars in the envelope and a note saying that the bill had already been paid. I wasn't to worry about the money, but to just keep preaching on the "net."

What did I do when I woke up? I worried about the money! Over time, whenever I "returned to the Lord," He reminded me that this was His idea, that He was with me, and that He had a plan for my future.

Because I returned to Him so many times to get this reminder, I finally took a red mesh grapefruit bag and put it in my bill drawer. Every time I'd worry about the money, I'd open that drawer, see the "net" and immediately sense the peace of God. There was nothing magical about the bag—it was simply a visual reminder of the promises God had made to me—but it helped me get through more than a few of my own "Wednesdays."

Don't let "Wednesdays" get you down. Don't let the rest of your week drop; don't let the rest of your marriage or job or children drop; don't let the rest of your life drop. Return to the Lord. He'll help you fight both battles. Remember: Friday's coming!

Lesson 8

GOD SETS PEOPLE FREE SO ALL WILL KNOW

Scripture Reading: Exodus 7-10

People sometimes wonder why God "hardens" Pharaoh's heart in the process of setting the Israelites free from Egypt. Why does God have to do it this way? Doesn't this override Pharaoh's free will, if God is the one who makes Pharaoh's heart hard?

Not at all! A friend of mine compares this to the different effects the sun has on two different objects: butter and clay. What happens when the sun shines on a lump of butter for a few hours? It gets soft. But what happens when the sun shines on a lump of clay for a few hours? It gets hard! The same sun that softens the butter, hardens the clay. The difference is not in the sun, but in the reaction of the objects to the sun.

When God pours out the plagues in Exodus chapters 7, 8, 9 and 10, Moses and Pharaoh have two different reactions. Moses' heart gets softer to God's purposes and Pharaoh's just gets harder and harder.

But there's still a deeper question in this story: Why does God have to bother with Moses, Pharaoh and the plagues at all? If God wants to set the people free, why doesn't He just cut off their chains, open the gates of Egypt and walk the people out? Why, for that matter, does God free anyone the way He does?

Why wait until Daniel's already in the lion's den before saving him? Why wait for little David to come onto the scene before defeating Goliath? Why wait till Jonah's near the bottom of the ocean before sending a whale out to save him?

God tells us the answer in every one of these stories.

He sets people free in a way that the world will know that He is the Lord, so that others will put their faith in Him and be set free, too.

We can read this over and over again in the story of the plagues:

- *"...and the Egyptians will know that I am the LORD..." (Exodus 7:5)*

- *"...by this you will know that I am the LORD..." (Exodus 7:17)*
- *"...so that you may know there is no one like the LORD..." (Exodus 8:10)*
- *"...so that you will know that I, the LORD, am in this land." (Exodus 8:22)*
- *"...that my name might be proclaimed in all the earth." (Exodus 9:16)*

We can read this over and over again throughout the Bible.

When God sets Daniel free from the lion's den, He does it in a way that so impresses the king of that land that the king *"wrote a letter to all the peoples, nations and men of every language throughout the land...that in every part of my kingdom people must fear and reverence the God of Daniel" (from Daniel 6:25-27).*

When God gave David the victory over Goliath, He did it in a way that *"the whole world will know that there is a God in Israel" (from 1 Samuel 17:45-46).*

When God rescued Jonah from the depths of the ocean, He was able to get His message out to the people of Nineveh so that even the king of that city issued a proclamation to all the people in his land: *"Let everyone call urgently on God. Let them give up their evil ways and their violence. Who knows? God may yet relent and with compassion turn from his fierce anger so that we will not perish" (from Jonah 3:7-9).*

If you wonder why God does things the way He does, pray that God would soften your heart to the things He's trying to do. Pray that God would soften the hearts of your family and friends to the things He may be trying to do through you. Then trust Him that He really does want to set you and your family and friends free.

God may be waiting for just the right time, just the right place, and just the right circumstances so that others will know that He is the Lord, put their faith and trust in Him, and be set free, too.

Lesson 9

ULTIMATE VICTORY COMES FROM ULTIMATE SACRIFICE

Scripture Reading: Exodus 11

How free do you want to be? If you want to get a little bit free, you only have to make a little bit of sacrifice. But if you want to get totally free, you have to make a total sacrifice.

I've ridden on a few swings with my kids before and there's a bit of a thrill that comes with it. But one day I went on a 100 foot bungee swing with them and it was a totally different experience!

After my six year old son and I were pulled half-way up to the top, he asked "Are we there yet?" When we were pulled still higher and higher, he hung onto my arm tighter and tighter. When we got to the top, I counted to three before pulling the cord that would plunge us down the 100 foot drop:

One! Two! Three! Whewwwww! The sense of freedom that came in those next few seconds was overwhelming as we swung down and then back up again over the crowd below us.

Moses had the chance to get a little bit of freedom for the Israelite slaves in Egypt. Pharaoh offered Moses the chance to go into the desert for a few days with just the men. Moses said, "No." Then Pharaoh said Moses could go with the women and children, too, but just leave the animals behind. Moses refused. Each time Pharaoh offered a compromise, Moses held out for total freedom, because that's what God had promised him.

In Exodus chapter 11, God tells Moses that total freedom is just around the corner, but it wouldn't come without cost.

So Moses said, "This is what the LORD says: 'About midnight I will go throughout Egypt. Every firstborn son in Egypt will die, from the firstborn son of Pharaoh, who sits on the throne, to the firstborn son of the slave girl, who is at her hand mill, and all the firstborn of the cattle as well. There will be loud wailing throughout Egypt - worse than there has ever been or ever will be again. But among the Israelites not a dog will bark at any man or animal.' Then you will know that the

LORD makes a distinction between Egypt and Israel" (Exodus 11:4-7).

Ultimate victory comes only from ultimate sacrifice.

None of the Israelites' sons would die in this way, but God called upon them to make a sacrifice, too—of a lamb. When they put the blood of the lamb on the doorframes of their homes, the Angel of the Lord would "pass over" them and not kill their sons, because their sacrifice had already been made.

There are times when something has to die so something else can live.

I heard a woman speak one night about dying to ourselves so that God could live through us. She quoted Madame Guyon, a Christian who lived in France in the 1600's, who talked about this total surrender as "plunging your will into the depths of God's will, there to be lost forever."

I was enthralled by this vision. But a friend of mine, who had heard the same talk, was scared to death by it. He wasn't sure if he could trust God or not, and wasn't wanting to take the chance to find out.

I wasn't sure I wanted to do the bungee

swing, either, until I saw a sign on the ride that said, "100% safety." That's what I needed to know to enjoy the ride of my life. Maybe you're not sure you want to totally surrender everything in your life to Christ. Let me assure you that based on my experience, the experience of others, and most importantly, the words of God Himself in the Bible, that God is trustworthy. He loves you, cares about you, and has already made the ultimate sacrifice for you. Jesus is *"the Lamb of God, who takes away the sin of the world!" (John 1:29b).*

If you want a little bit of freedom, trust Jesus a little bit. But if you want total freedom, put your faith in Christ for everything in your life. Everything! Then you'll find out the truth of Jesus' words: *"if the Son sets you free, you will be free indeed! (John 8:36).*

Lesson 10

God Fulfills His Promises In Unforgettable Ways

Scripture Reading: Exodus 12

Can you imagine an event so memorable that people would still celebrate it 3,500 years later? Not 35, or 350, but 3,500 years later!?! The Passover was just such an event: the night the Israelites were set free from their bondage in Egypt.

We've already looked at one of the reasons God does things the way He does: so that the whole world will know that He is God, so they will put their faith in Him, too. But in this lesson, we see yet another reason: sometimes God fulfills His promises in a way that is so unforgettable that people will remember it for years to come.

When God called me into full-time ministry, He used a verse about the Passover to confirm it. I was asking God to confirm some things He was telling me were going to happen that day.

Two verses of scripture came to my mind:

Genesis 2:3 and Exodus 12:2. I didn't know what the verses said, so I looked up Genesis 2:3. It was about the first Sabbath Day. Assuming I must have heard wrong on that one, I turned to Exodus 12:2, which was about the first Passover. I began to write in my journal, "God, I don't get it," but before I finished the sentence, I felt like God said: "Like the Sabbath and the Passover were markers of special days, so today will mark a special day for you, Eric."

"What will it mark?" I asked.

"The beginning of your ministry," He answered.

God did what He promised to do that day, and within 48 hours I had quit my job and launched out into full-time ministry.

As memorable as that event was for me, it was minuscule compared to what God did for the Israelites on that first Passover night:

"Each man is to take a lamb for his family...year-old males without defect, and...slaughter them at midnight....take some of the blood and put it on the sides and tops of the doorframes of the houses where they eat the lambs...On that same night I will pass through Egypt and strike down every firstborn -

both men and animals - and I will bring judgment on all the gods of Egypt. I am the LORD. The blood will be a sign for you on the houses where you are; and when I see the blood, I will pass over you. No destructive plague will touch you when I strike Egypt. This is a day you are to commemorate; for the generations to come you shall celebrate it as a festival to the LORD - a lasting ordinance" (Exodus 12:3, 6, and 12-14).

And a lasting celebration it has become. When Jesus celebrated the Passover on the night before He died, the tradition was already 1,500 years old. You've probably celebrated it, even if you weren't fully aware of it, if you've ever taken communion, or the Lord's Supper. For it was during the Passover meal that Jesus took the bread and the cup and spoke these words:

"This is my body, which is for you; do this in remembrance of me...this cup is the new covenant in my blood. Do this whenever you drink it in remembrance of me" (1 Corinthians 11:24-25).

Just as the Old Covenant required a lamb to be sacrificed so the Israelites could go free, the New Covenant has the same requirement so that we can go free, except that Jesus is that lamb. The Bible says, *"For Christ, our Passover lamb, has been sacrificed"* (I Corinthians 5:7).

For all that the Israelites had to go through in Egypt—the hard labor, the waiting, the wailing all around them—their day of freedom was so memorable we still celebrate it 3,500 years later.

Are you waiting for God to do something in your life? Are you wondering why it has to take so long—why your labor might be getting harder not easier? It just might be that God is working things out in such a way that when He does fulfill His promises to you, He will do it in a way that is so unforgettable, that you—and everyone around you—will remember it for years.

Lesson 11

MARK THE DATE

Scripture Reading: Exodus 13:1-16

If you could live any day of your life over again—because it was so memorable—which day would you re-live? For me, I'd pick November 19th, 1988, the day I asked my wife, Lana, to marry me. It was perfect in every way, even including the brief rain shower that fell on us while we rode paddle boats at the Houston Zoo.

Some dates are so memorable that we think we'll never forget them. But as time passes, and life takes its unexpected turns, we can sometimes forget, or simply devalue, what God has done for us in the past. And when we forget, we tend to quickly lose ground on any freedom we had gained up to that point.

In the last ten lessons of this study, we looked at how the Israelites were finally able to get free from their bondage. In the next ten lessons, we're going to look at how to stay free, which can be just as important as getting free in the first place.

The first lesson for staying free is this: mark the date. Make a point to deliberately remember, from year to year, just what God has done for you. And not only for you to remember, but as an opportunity to remind those around you what God has done for you, too.

Here's what God told the Israelites to do in Exodus chapter 13:

> *"Then Moses said to the people, 'Commemorate this day, the day you came out of Egypt, out of the land of slavery, because the LORD brought you out of it with a mighty hand ... You must keep this ordinance at the appointed time year after year ... In days to come, when your son asks you, 'What does this mean?' say to him, 'With a mighty hand the LORD brought us out of Egypt, out of the land of slavery' ... and it will be like a sign on your hand and a symbol on your forehead that the LORD brought us out of Egypt with his mighty hand."*

God knew what the Israelites would be facing in the future. He knew that they may one day wonder if they had made the wrong decision, if maybe they should turn around and go back to Egypt, back into bondage. But if they could simply remember this night and the miraculous deliverance they experienced that could only be attributed to the hand of God, they would have the faith to keep moving forward - faith to endure any obstacle in the future.

Some people scoff at holidays, thinking they serve no purpose except to give people a day off of work. But to those who use these "holy" days well, they can be powerful reminders of what God has done, and provide "staying power" for those who have been set free.

Here in the United States, we celebrate a holiday called Thanksgiving, a day that was established when the first people who came to this land from overseas wanted to remember all that God had done for them. They had lost much in the process of coming to America, including many loved ones who didn't survive the trip and their first few months here. But rather than despair over what they had lost, they gave thanks for what they had found.

The day before I wrote this lesson was November 19th. Throughout the day, I took time to remember what happened on the day I proposed to Lana. I told my kids about it. I told her brother about it. I told her Dad about it. I bought her flowers. I love to relive that day in my mind for myself, and out loud for others, because I want to continually remember throughout my life what God has done for me.

Are you struggling to stay free? Wondering if it might be better to head back to Egypt? If so, try taking some time this week to remember some of the things God has done for you in the past. Mark those dates on your calendar. Celebrate them every year. Let them be "like a sign on your hand and a symbol on your forehead" of all that the Lord has done for you.

Lesson 12

God's Route Takes Time For Our Sake

Scripture Reading: Exodus 13:17-22

Have you ever been able to see exactly where you want to go, but it seems like it takes forever to get there? The more you walk towards it, the farther away it gets? That may not be an optical illusion. That may just be the hand of God at work.

I've been working on a project for several years. Every once in awhile I think I see the finish line just around the next turn. Then I realize that it wasn't the finish line at all, but just another marker along the way. God urges me on, and seems to send me on another lap around the track.

Why does God do that? Isn't He the One who called us to run this race in the first place and holds out the prize for us at the end? In Exodus chapter 13, God gives us at least one of the reasons He holds us back from reaching the finish line too soon.

When God promised the Israelites He would bring them into "the Promised Land," He set them free from Egypt and sent them on their way. But instead of sending them on the straightest route, He deliberately sent them on a much longer route around the desert. He tells us why in Exodus 13:17-18a:

"When Pharaoh let the people go, God did not lead them on the road through the Philistine country, though that was shorter. For God said, 'If they face war, they might change their minds and return to Egypt.' So God led the people around by the desert road toward the Red Sea."

The Israelites were so fresh out of Egypt that God knew that if they went straight to the Promised Land and had to do battle right away, they might have hightailed it right back to Egypt. God knew that Egypt was a much worse place for them to be and it wasn't where He wanted them to be at all. *For their own protection,* God took them on the longer route.

Oftentimes we get frustrated when we have to take the longer route. We cry out, "God, why is it taking so long for me to get there? Why is it taking so long to restore my marriage that I know You want restored? To get the job that I know you want me to have? To bring back the child that I know You want to bring back? To finish the project that I know You called me to do?"

It might be that God is waiting until we're ready to say with our whole heart: "OK, God, I'm ready to take on this battle no matter what. I'm going to fight for my marriage the way You want me to fight for it. I'm going to fight for my job, fight for my purpose, fight for my calling in life. I want to be able to stand firm in these things, God, so teach me everything I need to know before I get there, because if I get there too soon, I might hightail it back to Egypt."

Proverbs 3:5-6 tells us how we can get this kind of attitude: *"Trust in the LORD with all your heart and lean not on your own understanding; in all your ways acknowledge him, and he will make your paths straight."*

Sometimes the shortest route in the long run is the longest route in the short run.

Don't be frustrated when God says to take another lap around the track. Don't give up on what God's called you to do. Don't give in to the thinking that you'll never make it. Follow the example of the Apostle Paul: *"But one thing I do: Forgetting what is behind and straining toward what is ahead, I press on toward the goal to win the prize for which God has called me heavenward in Christ Jesus" (Philippians 3:13b-14).*

Tell God: "Father, I'm ready when You are. Whether I reach my goal today or sometime down the road, I'm still going to trust You no matter what. You've brought me this far. I know You'll bring me home."

Lesson 13

STAND FIRM

Scripture Reading: Exodus 14:1-14

What can you do when your back is up against the wall, when you can't go forward, and when you feel like God doesn't want you to go backward? Sometimes the best thing to do is the hardest thing to do: to "stand firm."

A few years ago, my family was moving from Texas to Illinois. We had a very short timeframe to sell our house and make the move. As I prayed about it, I felt God wanted us to make the move between February 15th and February 28th, a two week window of time—that was less than two months away.

I was fighting for my faith on this one. I felt I was supposed to sell the house without a realtor, which can often take longer than with a realtor, and I didn't have any time to lose. Then I got a letter from a realtor that almost totally undid my faith. It read:

"It's now been a couple of weeks since you

began trying to sell your house by yourself, and for your sake I do hope you will be successful—although the odds are not with you. I say this because currently in this area there are some 470 full-time real estate professionals who are working 7 days a week to sell homes like yours. Yet even with so many professionals on the job, it is still taking an average of 30-120 days to get a listed home sold. Now, if it takes 470 full-time professionals over 4 months to get a house sold, how long will it take you—working part-time by yourself?"

I wondered what to do. It was critical that we sell our house quickly. Then I was reminded of the Israelites in Exodus, chapter 14.

They had just been set free from Egypt when God led them right up to the edge of the Red Sea. Pharaoh had changed his mind again, wondering why he had let his slaves go free. He took his chariots and chased after the Israelites, threatening to put them into bondage again. The Israelites saw their captors coming and cried out to Moses:

"Was it because there were no graves in Egypt that

you brought us to the desert to die? What have you done to us by bringing us out of Egypt? Didn't we say to you in Egypt, 'Leave us alone; let us serve the Egyptians'? It would have been better for us to serve the Egyptians than to die in the desert!" (Exodus 14:11-12).

Sometimes we wonder the same thing. We finally get free from something that has enslaved us, then it tries to force its way back into our lives to captivate us again. We panic. We wonder why we ever tried to get free in the first place. But Moses told his people something that helped them stay free, and it can help us stay free as well. Moses answered:

"Do not be afraid. Stand firm and you will see the deliverance the LORD will bring you today. The Egyptians you see today you will never see again. The LORD will fight for you; you need only to be still" (Exodus 14:13-14).

Even Moses couldn't have guessed that God was going to part the Red Sea for them to cross, but he knew that God had brought them this far, and He could bring them home.

In my own small way, I felt like Moses with my back up against the Sea. I was about to panic when I got that realtor's letter. But I decided to "stand firm." As if in confirmation of my decision, I read another story in 1 Kings 18 where God answered the prayers of one man, Elijah, over the misguided prayers of 450 others. It was close enough to my situation up against the 470 realtors mentioned in the letter that it gave me goose bumps!

Three weeks later we had a buyer for the house. We finalized the sale on February 26th and pulled out of town on February 28th.

Standing orders are good orders. If God hasn't directed a change in your plans, the best plan is to "stand firm" in the plan He's already given you.

Don't give in to fear. Stand firm in God!

Lesson 14

TAKE ACTION

Scripture Reading: Exodus 14:15-31

In our last study, we took a look at "standing firm" when our back is up against the wall. In this study, we'll look at what to do next, because God doesn't want us to stand still forever. There comes a time when God calls us to take action.

To paraphrase a preacher in the early days of America, who had been praying about what God wanted him to do in regards to creating this new country: "There's a time to pray and a time to act. Now's the time to act!"

Prayer is not a one-way conversation, but is an invitation for God to speak. And when God speaks, we need to do what He says, no matter how trivial a thing he might tell us to do.

God spoke to Moses when Moses' back was up against the wall of the Red Sea. The people had been crying out to Moses, complaining that he had brought them out into the desert to die at the hands of the Egyptians. As the Egyptian chariots quickly approached, Moses told the people to "stand firm," and they would see the deliverance of the Lord.

But then God told Moses what to do next:
"Then the LORD said to Moses, 'Why are you crying out to me? Tell the Israelites to move on. Raise your staff and stretch out your hand over the sea to divide the water so that the Israelites can go through the sea on dry ground. ...' Then Moses stretched out his hand over the sea, and all that night the LORD drove the sea back with a strong east wind and turned it into dry land. The waters were divided, and the Israelites went through the sea on dry ground, with a wall of water on their right and on their left" (Exodus 14:15-16, 21-22).

Moses may have thought: *What? Just raise my staff and stretch out my hand over the sea? How could that help!?!* But Moses did what God said to do, and the Lord blew back the waters with His very breath, delivering the Israelites to safety and destroying their captors.

I was farming with my Dad one day when the rain began to fall on our two tractors. I

Take Action

was driving ahead of my Dad, preparing the ground so he could plant the grain behind me. It was critical that we got the crops in the ground that day. We didn't have time for a storm.

As the rain started hitting my face, I stood up on the open-air tractor, held my hand up above my head, and prayed that the rain would stop. Guess what happened? I got drenched! Totally soaked from head to toe! I said, "Okay, God, I don't have control over the wind and rain."

But as I thought about it some more, I said, "Even though I don't have control, God, I believe that You do. I think this is just Satan trying to discourage me. God, I'm going to put my hand back up and keep on praying. I'm going to keep driving and praying until the rain stops, because we need to get Dad's crops in today!"

Although the rain kept pelting me in the face, I held my hand up high. I was still getting soaked for a few more minutes, but by the time I got to the other end of the field and turned around to take another pass, the rain had completely stopped. For the rest of the day, we planted that field as the rain came down in sheets all around us. Even the cars that drove on the road bordering our field had their windshield wipers going all day long, but the rain didn't touch the ground we were planting.

God doesn't always answer our prayers so dramatically, and even when He doesn't, we can be assured that He has something better in mind for us, because God is ultimately FOR us.

But when God *does* tell you to take action, take action! No matter how big or how small that action may be, make sure to get it done. Don't let Satan get you down. Lift your hands to God and press on!

Lesson 15

TAKE TIME TO PRAISE GOD

Scripture Reading: Exodus 15:1-21

When you've broken free from something in your life, what's a practical thing you can do to stay free?

One thing is to write down specifically what God has done for you—in a poem, in a song, or just in some words that don't even rhyme. When you take the time to write it down, especially in a way that can be recited or sung later, those words can be a reminder of what God has done for you—and what He's going to do in the future.

I don't think of myself as a poet, but sometimes poems just come out! One came out when I was a senior in college when I was dating Lana. I was working at an office that had an Apple computer called the "Lisa." "Lisa" was Apple's forerunner to the Macintosh, and was the first of Apple's computers to have a "graphical user interface," years before Microsoft created "windows."

That's when I fell in love, not only with Lana, but also with Apple computers. I discovered that this computer allowed me to express myself in a poem by drawing pictures next to the text:

"I love your name Lana,
You don't look like a (I drew a picture of a banana).
Your (I drew a picture of her hair) is so curly,
You never look (I drew a picture of a squirrel) -ly."

I'll spare you from having to read the rest of the poem! As goofy as it was, Lana has kept it to this day.

The fact that we take the time to write down something about someone special can have a significant impact on them—and on us.

For the Israelites, when they got free from the Egyptians and made it to the other side of the Red Sea, they seemed to almost spontaneously combust into a song about the experience:

*"I will sing to the LORD,
for he is highly exalted.
The horse and its rider
he has hurled into the sea."*
(Exodus 15:1)

This goes on for 20 more verses. The song is specifically about their experience, recalling how the water piled up like a wall on each side of them, and then how God blew the water back into place again with His breath, plunging their enemies to the depths like a stone. The song then turns into a song of hope for what God promised to do for them in the future.

Their song was such a powerful reminder of God's deliverance that we still sing some of its refrains today, such as, "And I shall prepare him my heart..." from the song *Exodus XV*.

Just as people love it when we take time to write about how much they mean to us, God loves it, too. One of the reasons is because it takes time to write down the words. In that time, when we recall what God has done for us and what He has promised to do for us in the future, we can find hope to go on. We can remember all that He's done and all that He's going to do. We remind ourselves that we don't really want to go back to our own "Egypt" ever again.

As I wrote this lesson, we were about to celebrate Christmas all around the world. We were getting ready to sing songs about things that God has done throughout the ages, some of them thousands of years ago, and some just a few years ago. I wondered aloud if maybe it was time for a new song, too?

Has God done something in your life that you'd like to remember forever—something that you'd like to pass on to future generations? Or is there someone special in your life who could use a special gift this week? Not a gift from a store, but a gift from a storehouse of love. If so, let it flow! Write a poem to the awesome God we serve—or to someone that you love. If you like music, how about writing a tune, or just humming one that can go along with the poem?

Then give it to your Beloved as a special act of love. They'll keep it forever. And it will help keep you free!

Lesson 16

CRY OUT TO THE LORD

Scripture Reading: Exodus 15:22-27

What makes Christmas so special for so many people? I think the answer can be summed up in one word: JESUS. That one word contains more power, more hope and more love than all the others words in the world combined.

Even the word "Jesus" has a significant meaning. It comes from the Greek form of the name Joshua, which means "the Lord saves." So to say that "Jesus Saves" is like saying, in bold and underlined, "The Savior Saves!" It is the saving power of Jesus that makes Christmas so special to me and millions of others around the world.

It is that same Truth that God has been trying to get across to people for thousands of years.

Three thousand years ago there were over 600,000 men, women and children who were on the verge of death in the middle of a desert. They had just lived through some of the most fearful and awesome moments ever recorded in history, and yet they found themselves once again at the edge of calamity.

Having found no water in the desert for three days, they finally found water at a place called Marah—only to discover that the water was bitter and was undrinkable. This was the last straw. They grumbled to Moses, and Moses did the best thing any of us can do in such a situation—he cried out to the Lord:

> *"Then Moses cried out to the LORD, and the LORD showed him a piece of wood. He threw it into the water, and the water became sweet" (Exodus 15:25).*

Once again, "the Lord saves." There's a big difference between grumbling to others and crying out to the Lord. "Grumbling to others" is giving in to defeat and failure. "Crying out to the Lord" is looking up with hope and anticipation. The people grumbled. Moses cried out to the Lord, and the Lord showed him exactly what to do.

A man here in the U.S., by the name of George Washington Carver, saw poverty and desperation all around him in his home state of Georgia. He cried out to the Lord, asking God to show him the secrets of the universe. God told George that this would be too much for him to handle! So George asked God to show him the secrets of the peanut, an unimportant plant at that time that grew in Georgia. In response to that cry, God showed George hundreds of uses for the peanut, including peanut butter, oils, lubricants, paints and more. George put his wisdom to use and turned the peanut into a $13 million industry for the state of Georgia.

Back to Jesus, I heard from a woman who had grown up as a Buddhist, and who one day she found herself in the blackest of holes. Her marriage, her family, and her life were a total mess. She didn't know what to do. So she did the one thing she hadn't tried before. She called out to Jesus, whom she had heard about on television. Standing in the middle of her living room, she looked up to heaven, with tears in her eyes, and called out to Jesus as loud as she could. With that cry, Jesus totally and completely transformed her life here on earth and gave her a future in heaven, too. You can read her whole story on The Ranch website by going to "Stories" and clicking on "Jesus Get Me Out Of Here!"

I don't know where you are today or what you're going through. But the Lord knows—the Lord who saves, the Lord who took a truly desperate situation and completely turned it around by showing Moses the simplest of solutions—to throw a stick into bitter water to make it sweet.

What do you need from the Lord today? Don't grumble to others. Cry out to the Lord! Listen for His answer, no matter how simple. You might find that the solution is right under your nose. You just need the Lord to show it to you! You'll find out again that the Lord is able to save you and those around you, perhaps even hundreds of thousands around you! Remember what "Jesus" means: "The Lord Saves!"

Lesson 17

Trust God To Provide Showing He's The Lord

Scripture Reading: Exodus 16

Want to see the hand of God at work in your life this year? Try this: take time to write down each of your prayers in a journal or on a pad of paper. Then leave some space next to each prayer so that you can come back later to record when, and how, that prayer was answered.

Within just a few weeks, you'll begin to see how many prayers God answers on a regular basis. You'll also see how often He answers those prayers in a way that you'll *know* it was the Lord who answered them. By connecting your prayers to God's answers, you'll both see and know that God's hand is at work in your life.

This is how God said He would answer the prayers of the Israelites when they cried out for food in the desert in Exodus chapter 16:

The LORD said to Moses, "I have heard the

grumbling of the Israelites. Tell them, 'At twilight you will eat meat, and in the morning you will be filled with bread. Then you will know that I am the LORD your God' " (Exodus 16:11-12).

Starting the very next day, God gave them manna every morning and quail every night, not as the result of some natural desert phenomenon, but clearly as a result of God delivering on His promise exactly as He told them He would.

One day, God answered one of my prayers in a similarly specific way when I was praying about where God wanted me to live and minister.

I was living in Illinois at the time and had a map of the United States laying out on the table. Just out of curiosity, I closed my eyes and let my finger fall on the map. When I saw that it had landed on Dallas, Texas, I closed the map. I really wasn't wanting to go back to Texas again, since I had just moved back to Illinois from from Texas just a few years earlier.

But later that night, as I told a friend on the phone what had happened regarding the map, my friend immediately described to me a picture that God had impressed on his mind when I said the word "Dallas." He described a place called "The Ranch," not the famous ranch from the old TV show "Dallas," but a scene he had never seen before. He told me in detail about the location of the trees, the sunset, some obstacles, a dirt path, a fence, and a river by, next to which stood one solitary tree casting its shadow on the water.

My friend drew what he had seen on a piece of paper. He signed it, dated it and faxed me a copy. Vision or no vision, I still wasn't interested in going to Texas! So I promptly forgot about it....until several months later when I got a phone call from a pastor in Dallas, Texas. He wanted to know if I would be interested in moving to Dallas to serve as the Associate Pastor at his church. I had to pull out my friend's sketch and ask God if there was any connection between the call and my earlier prayer. It turns out there was! You can see the whole story on *The Ranch* website by watching the video for this lesson.

Suffice it to say we ended up moving to Dallas! Exactly one year later—to the day—I found myself standing on the bank of the river outside our new back yard, looking at a scene that had been detailed a year earlier in a drawing I now held in my hand and included the trees, the sunset, the obstacles, the dirt path, the fence, and even the solitary tree casting its shadow onto the water! To top it all off, just behind this scene was a brand new sports rehab center that happened to open that very month called, "The Ranch." (This story was the inspiration for how I decided to call my website *The Ranch!*)

If you want to see the hand of God at work in your life, take time to write down your prayers—then leave room for His answers! When you make the connection between your prayers and God's answers, you'll begin to see clearly that the Lord really is "the LORD!"

Lesson 18

TAKE IT TO THE LORD

Scripture Reading: Exodus 17:1-7

What can we do when people seem to love us one minute and hate us the next—when we haven't even done anything differently? We can learn a lesson from Moses and do what he did: take it to the Lord.

I remember a man who had heard about some of the things I was doing in my walk of faith with God. He was so impressed that he came over to my house one day said to me: "you're the closest thing to a disciple I've ever seen." Within a month, that same man started to deride and question everything I did. I wasn't doing anything differently, but somehow his perception of me had changed during that month.

People can be fickle—and sometimes with good reason. But we still need to know how to respond to them. Moses had to deal with people's fickle reactions all the time. When things were going great in the camp, the people put their faith in Moses, following him wherever he led. But when circumstances changed, their opinions of Moses changed, even to the point where they wanted to stone him to death.

In Exodus 17, when the people found themselves without water again, they turned on Moses again:

> *"The whole Israelite community set out from the Desert of Sin, traveling from place to place as the LORD commanded. They camped at Rephidim, but there was no water for the people to drink. So they quarreled with Moses and said, 'Give us water to drink.'*
> *"Moses replied, 'Why do you quarrel with me? Why do you put the LORD to the test?' But the people were thirsty for water there, and they grumbled against Moses. They said, 'Why did you bring us up out of Egypt to make us and our children and livestock die of thirst?' " (Exodus 17:1-3).*

What could Moses do? Instead of taking it personally, he took it to the Lord—and the Lord answered him.

> *"Then Moses cried out to the LORD, 'What am I to do with these people? They are almost ready to stone me.'*
> *"The LORD answered Moses, 'Walk on ahead of the people. Take with you some of the elders of Israel and take in your hand the staff with which you struck the Nile, and go. I will stand there before you by the rock at Horeb. Strike the rock, and water will come out of it for the people to drink.' So Moses did this in the sight of the elders of Israel. And he called the place Massah and Meribah because the Israelites quarreled and because they tested the LORD saying, 'Is the LORD among us or not?' " (Exodus 17:4-7).*

This last question is the key question for all of us: "Is the Lord among us or not?" If we can answer that question, we can be dead to compliments and dead to criticism.

When God answered Moses, He clearly told Moses what to do: walk on ahead of the people, take some of the elders with him, along with his staff, with which God had already displayed his power. Then He told Moses: "I will stand there before you by the rock at Horeb."

God said, in effect: "Moses, I am with you.

Strike the rock and you'll have water for all the people."

Jesus said similar words to his disciples, words which still apply to all of us who call ourselves his disciples today: *"And surely I am with you always, to the very end of the age" (Matthew 28:20b).*

When we know that God is with us, we can properly respond to people's comments, whether they are compliments or criticism. The key is not in ignoring people's compliments or criticism, but in fully recognizing that God is with us in what we're doing. When we know that He is with us, we will clearly defer people's compliments *and* criticism to Him, knowing that it is God who is calling the shots, not us.

Whether people compliment you or criticize you, don't take it personally. Take it to the Lord, letting Him reassure you that He's still with you!

Lesson 19

Take Your Position And Maintain Your Position

Scripture Reading: Exodus 17:8-16

What difference can it make to those around you whether or not you can "stay up" in your faith? For some people, it may mean the difference between victory and defeat, between staying free and falling back into bondage.

When God calls us to take action, He wants us to take our position, and maintain our position, even when we begin to feel weak. He may even send others to help us so we can continue to stand strong.

In the case of Moses, God sent two men to help him when he was feeling weak. When Moses was wearing out, he lowered his arms, and his army began to lose. But when Aaron and Hur gave him a boost, Moses' army got a boost at the same time. There's a short description of this event in Exodus 17:

"The Amalekites came and attacked the Israelites

at Rephidim. Moses said to Joshua, 'Choose some of our men and go out to fight the Amalekites. Tomorrow I will stand on top of the hill with the staff of God in my hands.'

"*So Joshua fought the Amalekites as Moses had ordered, and Moses, Aaron and Hur went to the top of the hill. As long as Moses held up his hands, the Israelites were winning, but whenever he lowered his hands, the Amalekites were winning. When Moses' hands grew tired, they took a stone and put it under him and he sat on it. Aaron and Hur held his hands up—one on one side, one on the other—so that his hands remained steady till sunset. So Joshua overcame the Amalekite army with the sword*" (Exodus 7:8-13).

It must have seemed odd for Moses to tell Joshua to go into battle while Moses himself went up on a hill, holding his staff in his hands. But they both had their roles to play. They both had to take their positions and maintain their positions for victory to come. Moses needed to keep his staff in the air, and Joshua needed to fight with all his might.

What's the deal with Moses having to hold his arms up in the air? What good could that do? While I'm sure there were supernatural things that God did by having Moses raise his staff, (like turning water into blood and splitting the Red Sea in two), I also think there were some "natural" things that God did through this act, too.

As Joshua and the army looked up to the hill, they could see their leader, Moses, with his staff in his hands raised up to heaven. They could also see if Moses grew weary and lowered his arms. While one movement gave them strength and courage, the other movement led to weakness and discouragement.

Moses, Aaron and Hur all saw the effect this had on Joshua and the army. They knew what needed to be done. When Moses couldn't do it by himself anymore, Aaron and Hur stepped in to lift his hands for him. As they watched Joshua and the army until sunset that day, they saw the result of what they were doing: the Israelites were finally able to overcome the Amalekites.

A famous Christian once told his friend that he didn't want to be a role model for others. His friend said, "It's not a matter of whether or not you want to be a role model. You are a role model. The question is whether you're going to be a good role model or a bad one."

There are times when we may not feel like taking the position God has called us to take. There are times when we may not feel like maintaining the position God has called us to take. We may wish we could go down to fight instead of standing on a hill. Or we may wish we could go stand on a hill instead of going down to fight! But if God has called us to our position, we just need to take it and maintain it.

What position has God called you to take? Take your position and maintain your position —then watch to see the difference it can make in your life, and in the lives of those around you.

Lesson 20

TAKE THE ELDERS WITH YOU

Scripture Reading: Exodus 17:5-6

Has God ever called you to take a risky step of faith in front of other people? Why does He do that?

I know I'd rather take a risky step of faith when I'm all alone, in private, with no one watching. Sometimes we're able to do that, but there are other times when God calls us to take steps of faith with others looking on.

With today's lesson, we're turning a corner in the book of Exodus. In the first ten lessons, we looked at how to "get free" from the bondages in our life. In lessons 11-20, we covered how to "stay free" once we've gotten free. In the next ten lessons, we're going to look at how to "set others free," a big part of which involves enlisting the help of others.

Take a look at how God begins to do this here in Exodus chapter 17:

"The LORD answered Moses, 'Walk on ahead of

the people. Take with you some of the elders of Israel and take in your hand the staff with which you struck the Nile, and go. I will stand there before you by the rock at Horeb. Strike the rock, and water will come out of it for the people to drink'" (Exodus 17:5-6).

Why did God tell Moses to take some of the elders of Israel with him on his way to strike the rock?

Although the text of this chapter doesn't say specifically, we can get an idea of what might be going on by looking ahead at the next few chapters. Moses' father-in-law is about to come onto the scene and tell Moses to divide up the work of leading the people, encouraging Moses to choose leaders over groups of tens, hundreds and thousands to help share the leadership load. The elders that go with Moses to the rock are likely to be some of the same elders who will take on these new roles.

While taking our steps of faith in private may be "safe," taking those same steps in public may be significant in helping others take their own steps of faith down the road.

When I began my Internet ministry, I

reached a point where I was overwhelmed with requests for prayer and advice. So I invited some people to help me respond to all the emails that were coming in. One of those who volunteered was a woman from Tennessee who had a heart, and a gift, for helping people. Over the years of helping us, her burden for helping others over the Internet continued to grow.

The week that I wrote this lesson, she launched an Internet ministry of her own at www.DayByDay7.org. Taking what she has learned about doing ministry over the Internet and combining it with her other God-given gifts and talents, she's now poised to help many more people grow in their faith. Here's part of a note I got from her that week:

"I just wanted to share with you that I got my first prayer request from someone in California. I don't even know how they got my website. I can't tell you how hard that hit me —it was so sudden and I didn't expect to get any hits or prayer requests so soon. It was completely awesome. You should have seen me praising the Lord. All the hard work was worth it! At that moment, the poem on my website came to pass: if I can ease one pain, it will all be worth it!"

The closing of her note tied together this idea of the value of taking others with us while we step out in faith. She wrote: "Thank you for allowing me to volunteer with The Ranch and for encouraging me to reach out to others through your ministry and this one. I don't know where God will take it, but I'm ready! You are my inspiration for DayByDay7.org."

Why does God call us to sometimes take steps of faith with others watching? Perhaps one of the reasons is so that when we walk along with each other, we can encourage each other to keep taking more steps of faith, thus expanding the ministry of "setting others free."

Lesson 21

Put A System In Place

Scripture Reading: Exodus 18

Feeling overwhelmed with too much to do? Don't despair. Help may be on the way! I was lamenting to a friend one day about all the things I felt God wanted me to do. She asked: "Why would God give you more to do than one person could do?" I knew the answer: He wouldn't. He knows what I can handle and what I can't.

So I knew there were only two options left: 1) Either God *hadn't* given me everything I felt He wanted me to do, and I needed to back out of some of them; Or 2) God *had* given me all the things I felt He wanted me to do, and I needed to find a new way to do them.

It turned out to be some of both. For this lesson, though, I want to focus on the second option. There *are* times when God calls us to accomplish things for Him, that don't require us to do them all by ourselves.

Moses found himself in this situation when leading over 600,000 men, not counting all the women and children, through a desert. Moses' father-in-law, Jethro, saw all that Moses was doing and said:

> *"What is this you are doing for the people? Why do you alone sit as judge, while all these people stand around you from morning till evening?"*
> *Moses answered him, "Because the people come to me to seek God's will. Whenever they have a dispute, it is brought to me, and I decide between the parties and inform them of God's decrees and laws."*
> *Moses' father-in-law replied, "What you are doing is not good. You and these people who come to you will only wear yourselves out. The work is too heavy for you; you cannot handle it alone. Listen now to me and I will give you some advice, and may God be with you. You must be the people's representative before God and bring their disputes to him. Teach them the decrees and laws, and show them the way to live and the duties they are to perform. But select capable men from all the people— men who fear God, trustworthy men who hate dishonest gain—and appoint them as officials over thousands, hundreds, fifties and tens. Have them*

Put A System In Place

serve as judges for the people at all times, but have them bring every difficult case to you; the simple cases they can decide themselves. That will make your load lighter, because they will share it with you. If you do this and God so commands, you will be able to stand the strain, and all these people will go home satisfied."
Moses listened to his father-in-law and did everything he said. (Exodus 18:14-24)

Here was Moses, a man truly called by God to lead the people, yet becoming overwhelmed by taking care of every dispute by himself. Jethro saw that this would eventually wear Moses out—as well as all the people. So Jethro gave Moses some practical advice: "Get help!" Moses did, and he was able to fulfill the call of God on his life in a way that he was able to "stand the strain," and all the people went home "satisfied."

Was Moses called to lead the people? Absolutely. Did that mean he had to meet every need personally? Not at all. While he was still ultimately responsible for the people, he found that by putting a system into place and enlisting the help of others he was able to fulfill the call of God on his life.

If you're feeling overwhelmed with too much to do, it's worth an honest prayer to God: "Am I doing the things You want me to do? And if so, is there another way You want me to do them?" Then listen to His honest answers, which come at times through other people.

Even Moses, as close as He was to God, still allowed God to speak into His life through another human being. God's goal was to meet the needs of the people. Moses' goal was to see that it got done. Take a look at the goal, then look at your role. In the end, I believe God will help you to "stand the strain," and all the people will go home "satisfied."

Lesson 22

LET GOD ESTABLISH YOU IN PEOPLE'S EYES

Scripture Reading: Exodus 19

How many people will be affected by what you do this week? Chances are, it will be more people than any of us might realize.

We all have a "sphere of influence," people with whom we have contact throughout the week, people who can be influenced by the way we live our lives. It may include people in our own family, people where we work, or people where we just hang out. It may include a bank teller, a postal worker, a doctor, a nurse or a receptionist. It may include people at church, people on the Internet, or people we don't even know, who are watching what we do.

And what we do matters.

Take a look at what happened when Moses was obedient to God's call on his life, taking steps of faith even when surrounded by doubt. When God spoke to Moses from the burning bush, and called him to set the Israelites free, Moses hesitated to believe it. But God assured Moses that he was the man. To confirm it, God told Moses He would give him a sign:

"I will be with you. And this will be the sign to you that it is I who have sent you: When you have brought the people out of Egypt, you will worship God on this mountain" (Exodus 3:2).

Now if I were Moses, I think I would have been a little bit frustrated that the sign would only come *after* I had taken this huge step of faith! Why would God wait until *after* the Israelites were free, and worshiping Him back at this same mountain, to give Moses "the sign"?

To see why, fast forward several months. In Exodus chapter 19, we see that the sign wasn't just for Moses, but also for those in Moses' new sphere of influence.

When Moses stepped out in faith, and the people came back to the mountain to worship God, that became a sign that anyone could read. As the people gathered there at the foot of the mountain, God told Moses to remind the people:

> *"You yourselves have seen what I [God] did to Egypt, and how I carried you on eagles' wings and brought you to myself. Now if you obey me fully and keep my covenant, then out of all nations you will be my treasured possession."*
> *The people heard this and responded together, "We will do everything the LORD has said."*

Then God speaks these words to Moses:

> *"I am going to come to you in a dense cloud, so that the people will hear me speaking with you and will always put their trust in you' " (from Exodus 19:3-9).*

God wasn't done with Moses when they got to the mountain. God still had many years of work ahead for him, and God needed the people to always put their trust in Moses so that they would follow his lead.

Sometimes the signs God gives us are not just for us, but for others to read, too. When we step out in faith, being obedient to what

God has called us to do, it releases others to step out in faith and obedience as well.

A few years ago, I felt God wanted me to head up a city-wide outreach here in town. With more than a little fear in my heart, I finally brought up the idea at our local ministers' meeting. Within a year, we had over 200 people involved in planning and pulling off this event.

Looking back, I realized that my stepping out in faith, and doing what God had called me to do, was a catalyst for others to step out in faith, and do what God had called them to do.

People are affected by what we do.

What is God calling you to do? Remember that you may not be the only one who is affected by what you do or don't do. None of us live in isolation. In fact, the sign that God gives you to show that He really is with you may just be the sign someone else needs to read! Then they'll be able to see that God is with them, too!

Lesson 23

Rules Can Be Good!

Scripture Reading: Exodus 20:1-21

How do you like rules? If you're like most people, you probably love rules—for other people, anyway! Rules keep people from stealing our stuff, running into us when we go through intersections, and harming those we love.

But what about rules for ourselves? Many times, we balk at rules. They make us feel restricted and constrained. But the rules God has set into place are the best kind of rules. They're helpful for us *and* for others. Instead of constricting us, they set us free to live the best life possible.

Without rules, I would be like a train without a track, or a kite without a string. If I were a train, I would think that the track was constraining me from going where I wanted to go. But in reality, the track would be the very thing that enabled me to go at all—and to go far and fast! If I were a kite, I would think that the string would be holding me back. But in reality, the tension of the string is the very thing that would help me to go higher and stay up longer than if I were to cut myself loose from it!

Exodus chapter 20 lists the most helpful and enduring set of rules ever given to anyone: The Ten Commandments. Thousands of years later, they still form the basis for many legal systems throughout the world.

> *"And God spoke all these words:*
> *'I am the LORD your God, who brought you out of Egypt, out of the land of slavery. You shall have no other gods before me.'*
> *'You shall not make for yourself an idol in the form of anything in heaven above or on the earth beneath or in the waters below. You shall not bow down to them or worship them; for I, the LORD your God, am a jealous God, punishing the children for the sin of the fathers to the third and fourth generation of those who hate me, but showing love to a thousand generations of those who love me and keep my commandments.'*
> *'You shall not misuse the name of the LORD your God, for the LORD will not hold anyone guiltless who misuses his name.'*

'Remember the Sabbath day by keeping it holy. Six days you shall labor and do all your work, but the seventh day is a Sabbath to the LORD your God. On it you shall not do any work, neither you, nor your son or daughter, nor your manservant or maidservant, nor your animals, nor the alien within your gates. For in six days the LORD made the heavens and the earth, the sea, and all that is in them, but he rested on the seventh day. Therefore the LORD blessed the Sabbath day and made it holy.'

'Honor your father and your mother, so that you may live long in the land the LORD your God is giving you.'

'You shall not murder.'

'You shall not commit adultery.'

'You shall not steal.'

'You shall not give false testimony against your neighbor.'

'You shall not covet your neighbor's house. You shall not covet your neighbor's wife, or his manservant or maidservant, his ox or donkey, or anything that belongs to your neighbor' " (Exodus 20:1-17).

Rather than restricting us, these rules free

us to live the abundant life God created us to live.

Now step back a minute and look at these rules from God's perspective. Why did He give these rules to Moses at this particular point in the journey out of Egypt? Based on Moses' recent conversation with Jethro, I believe it was God's way to teach everyone His decrees and laws, and to show them the way to live, as Jethro suggested in Exodus 18:20. At this critical point, God gave Moses a detailed set of rules to pass on to others so they could help him lead.

If you're wondering how to lead others better, or if you're wondering how you can live a more abundant life yourself, consider putting a good set of rules into place. A good set of rules, like a train track and a kite string, can often help us go farther and faster, and to fly longer and higher than ever before!

Lesson 24

SHARE WHAT YOU'VE LEARNED WITH OTHERS

Scripture Reading: Exodus 20:22-23:19

What has God taught you that might be helpful to others? We've all learned things from Him over the years—things we've done wrong, things we've done right, things He's spoken to us or through us.

I was in the midst of writing down some of the things God had spoken to me when I was reading Exodus chapters 20, 21, 22 and 23. When I read about God's conversation with Moses on the mountain, and how God gave Moses the Ten Commandments and the 600+ rules that followed, I saw what God was doing in a new light.

Of course, we're supposed to read what God spoke to Moses during those forty days, and of course, we'll be blessed if we follow that wisdom. But I also saw a new lesson for my life when I stepped back and looked at what God was doing overall. God was pouring out His wisdom to Moses so that Moses could pour it out to others.

The lesson for me was that God has poured out wisdom into our lives, too, and He wants us to pour it out to others.

Up to this point in the story of how God set the Israelites free from Egypt, Moses was the sole judge over the entire nation. Everyone who had a dispute would bring it to Moses to be settled. God would give Moses the wisdom he needed to make a ruling, and Moses would make the decision.

This worked for a time, but eventually it began to wear Moses and the people out. So God, through the words of Jethro, prompted Moses to delegate the work of judging others to several of the other leaders of Israel. Moses would still be available to hear the most difficult cases, but the majority of cases could be decided by these others.

It was at this time—as Moses prepared to delegate these duties—that God called Moses up to the mountain and spoke to him the Ten Commandments and all the rules that followed. As I read through this list of commandments, I could almost picture how the conversation between God and Moses might have gone:

"Moses, do you remember when that bull gored a man to death—the bull that had never gored anyone before? And do you remember how I told you to rule in that situation—that the bull must be killed, but the owner of the bull would not be held responsible? Share that with others.

"And do you remember when another bull gored a man to death, but that bull had a habit of goring people? Do you remember how I told you to rule in that situation—that the bull must be killed as well as the owner, unless those hurt by the goring would accept payment from the owner instead? Share that, too."

Although the actual conversation between God and Moses isn't recorded, the result of what God spoke during those forty days *is* recorded. What should be done when a bull gores someone is clearly spelled out in Exodus 21:28-32.

Maybe God reminded Moses of things that happened in the past, as well as telling him about things that might come up in the future. God spoke to Moses about all kinds of topics one by one, from cases involving adultery, theft and murder, to love, lust and anger. Then God asked Moses to share them with others, which he did.

Now, thousands of years later, we can still read these words of wisdom that came from the mouth of God. They form the foundation of the laws that are currently on the books in country after country. They help us to understand our basic rights, how to get along with each other, and how to better love God and our neighbors.

Think with me for a minute how this lesson might apply to you.

God has spent a lifetime pouring out His wisdom into you. What topics in life has God spoken to you about the most? Or the most often? Or the most clearly? What questions have you struggled with, wrestled through, and found God's answers?

Take time to share what you've learned with others. The answers you' found may set them free, too.

Lesson 25

Little By Little

Scripture Reading: Exodus 23:20-33

Praying for anything big to happen in your life? Waiting for God to bring it about? Wondering why it's not coming about as fast as you'd like?

When I get frustrated that I'm not seeing the big, grand vision come together for something that I really think God is putting on my heart, I take comfort from a short passage in Exodus chapter 23. It reminds me that God is able "to do immeasurably more than all we can ask or imagine," as the New Testament says in Ephesians 3:20, but that God doesn't always do it all at once.

Why not? Here's what God told the Israelites, and what He often tells me, too.

As the Israelites approached the "promised land," a huge expanse of property that God promised to give them when they got out of Egypt, God told them that He would drive out the current occupants of the land because of their wickedness and rebellion against Him. But, He added:

> *"I will not drive them out in a single year, because the land would become desolate and the wild animals too numerous for you. Little by little I will drive them out before you, until you have increased enough to take possession of the land" (Exodus 23:29-30).*

God was still going to give them their promised land, but little by little, for their own protection, and for the safekeeping of His vision for the land.

Even though there were over 600,000 Israelites at the time, the land was still bigger than they could effectively manage had they gotten it all at once. The land would have become desolate and overrun with wild animals. God, in His grace, was going to wait to drive out the current inhabitants until the Israelites increased enough to take possession of the land.

This is extremely encouraging to me! I don't like to wait for God's promises to be fulfilled—especially when I can see them so clearly, when they look like they're within reach, yet when I can't seem to take hold of them. These verses remind me that God *will* do what He says He will do, but in *His* timing, for *our* good and *for the good of the vision He's given us.*

For many years now I've been praying for a real "ranch," a place where I can invite people to spend time with God, away from the busy-ness of their lives. I've been to just such a ranch with my family—a beautiful private retreat on 240 acres of rolling hills in northern Illinois. Yet as I looked around at the expanse of the property, I couldn't imagine all of the care and maintenance it would take just to put gravel on the back roads every few years, let alone take care of all the cattle, sheep, ducks, fencing and guest homes.

Even though this seems to be exactly what I've been praying for, and continue to pray for, I know that I've not "increased enough to take possession" of the fullness of this vision. That doesn't stop me from asking, and it doesn't stop me from believing that God will someday fulfill the fullness of what He's put on my heart. But it does help me to be thankful—so thankful—that God holds back from giving me what I'm asking for before I can handle it.

Maybe you've been praying for some big things to happen in your life, or a friend's life. Maybe you've wondered why things aren't happening as fast as you'd like, or to the extent that you'd like. Maybe you're getting discouraged and wondering why God is poking around, taking His time, when there are so many things you want to get done—and now!

Take heart from this little passage in Exodus 23. As God Himself says several times in this passage, He *will* do what He promised. There are still things He wants us to do in the mean time. But, for our benefit, and for the benefit of His unfolding vision, He often carries out His will "little by little"—so we won't be overwhelmed by the answer when it does come.

Lesson 26

Come Up To The Lord And Worship

Scripture Reading: Exodus 24

What's the ultimate goal of being set free? What does freedom finally allow us to do, without hindrance?

The answer I've read over and over in Scripture is this: we're set free so we can worship God.

If a person can't worship God, fully from their heart, then they're still in bondage. They may live in a free country, but if they can't worship God, they're not really free at all. On the other hand, they may live in a prison cell, but if they can worship God, they are truly free. The degree of freedom we have in our lives is directly proportional to the degree to which we're able to worship God from our hearts.

This was God's ultimate goal for setting the Israelites free from Egypt. He told Moses to bring the people out into the desert so they could worship Him. He sets us free from sin, not only because it's good and helpful for us, but also so that we can be released to worship Him with our whole hearts.

In Exodus 24, Moses and his people have finally made it out to the place where God told Moses to come. Now they can start doing what they came to do, starting with Moses and some of the other leaders. God calls them up to the mountain to worship. The rest of the people will get their chance soon. But for now, God calls Moses to lead the way:

"Then he said to Moses, 'Come up to the LORD, you and Aaron, Nadab and Abihu, and seventy of the elders of Israel. You are to worship at a distance, but Moses alone is to approach the LORD; the others must not come near. And the people may not come up with him' " (Exodus 24:1-2).

Moses is about to become their "worship leader."

And what a worship service it is! Take a look at what happens when they come up to the Lord:

"Moses and Aaron, Nadab and Abihu, and the seventy elders of Israel went up and saw the God of

Israel. Under his feet was something like a pavement made of sapphire, clear as the sky itself. But God did not raise his hand against these leaders of the Israelites; they saw God, and they ate and drank." (Exodus 24:9-10).

They saw God—and lived! Then they ate and drank in His presence there on the mountain. Wow! To come into the presence of God, to see Him, to eat and drink and have a party right there at His feet—that's a true mountaintop experience!

The cool thing is, *we* can now do that any day of the week, no matter where we are or what's going on in our lives. We can take a moment, even right now, today, to spend a few minutes in the presence of the Lord, worshiping Him in our hearts.

You may not be able to sing. You may not be able to play an instrument. You may not be able to speak well. But you can do one thing right now that no one can stop you from doing: you can worship God in your heart.

You might not think you can. You might think other's are hindering you from it. You might think your circumstances are preventing it. But the truth is, nothing—and no one—can stop you from worshiping God. You can choose right now to worship Him!

Just say, "Father, I want to worship You. I want to be in Your presence. I want to eat and drink and enjoy a few moments with You, right now. I want to worship You!"

If sin is holding you back, confess it. If fear is getting you off track, let the Lord, Your shepherd, lead you beside His still waters. If life is weighing you down, let Jesus pick you up. He offered each of us this promise: *"Come to me, all you who are weary and burdened, and I will give you rest" (Matthew 11:28).*

Come up to the Lord and worship. This is why He set you free!

Lesson 27

GOD CAN SPEAK SPECIFICALLY AND CLEARLY

Scripture Reading: Exodus 25:1-27:19

Do you ever wonder if God speaks to people? And if so, does He just speak in generalities, giving us good principles to live by, but leaving the details up to us?

I was in a Bible study with a friend who felt that God does speak to us, but only in terms of giving us the "big picture." The specifics were for us to figure out. I understood what my friend was saying—and at times that is certainly true.

But as I've read through the Bible, I've also been struck by how often God speaks to people with very specific instructions—instructions that He wants to be followed precisely —even down to the last "cubit."

Exodus chapters 25, 26, and 27 are prime examples of God speaking specifically and clearly. In the opening words of chapter 25, God tells Moses to collect some very specific items from the people: ram skins dyed red, acacia wood, onyx stones and more. God continues with these words:

"Then have them make a sanctuary for me, and I will dwell among them. Make this tabernacle and all its furnishings exactly like the pattern I will show you" (Exodus 25:8-9).

For the next 89 verses, God gave Moses a detailed description of exactly how to build this tabernacle, and all of the elements within it: the ark of the covenant, the tables, the lampstands, the altars, the oil, the shovels— even the meat forks.

Listen to some of this detail:

... "Make a lampstand of pure gold and hammer it out, base and shaft; its cups, buds and blossoms shall be of one piece with it. Six branches are to extend from the sides of the lampstand—three on one side and three on the other. Three cups shaped like almond flowers with buds and blossoms are to be on one branch, three on the next branch, and the same for all six branches extending from the lampstand" (Exodus 25:31-33).
... "Make the tabernacle with ten curtains of finely

twisted linen and blue, purple and scarlet yarn, with cherubim worked into them by a skilled craftsman. All the curtains are to be the same size—twenty-eight cubits long and four cubits wide" (Exodus 26:1-2).

... *"Build an altar of acacia wood, three cubits high; it is to be square, five cubits long and five cubits wide.... Make a grating for it, a bronze network, and make a bronze ring at each of the four corners of the network. Put it under the ledge of the altar so that it is halfway up the altar"* (Exodus 27:1,4-5).

The detail reminds me of when God told Noah precisely how to build the ark for the animals, describing its dimensions cubit by cubit (a length of about 18 inches).

Why was God so specific? Maybe it was because there had never been a need for a boat like that before. How could Noah have known how many animals would show up? It was better for Noah to follow God's specific instructions up front on how to build the ark, than to try to build it his own way and then have the elephants and hippos and rhinos and giraffes show up!

When we need wisdom, we can ask God

for it. He's the Creator of the universe. He knows how every molecule is put together. He knows what needs to be done and how to do it. And He's glad to pour out that wisdom into us.

The Bible says: *"If any of you lacks wisdom, he should ask God, who gives generously to all without finding fault, and it will be given to him" (James 1:5).*

God *can* speak specifically and clearly. There's no doubt about it scripturally, as in this case from Exodus. Someone might wonder, based on their experience (or lack thereof), if God speaks specifically. But based on Scripture, there's no doubt that He does!

Whatever you're working on right now—a project for work, a new type of ministry, a relationship with a spouse, child or friend—ask God for wisdom on how to proceed. Then listen, and do, what He says!

Lesson 28

GIVE DIGNITY & HONOR TO THOSE SERVING WITH YOU

Scripture Reading: Exodus 27:20-28:40

What can we do to give dignity and honor to those who serve with us? And what difference can it make when we do?

I once attended a church that was very formal. All the pastors wore black robes. At one point, one of the pastors wanted to start preaching in just his suit, without the robe. He wanted to be less formal so that the people he was trying to reach would feel he was more like them.

But some of the leaders of the church didn't like that idea. It went against their particular view of church life. While the church eventually let him preach without his robe for the first of their three morning worship services, he had to put it on again for the other two services.

I thought the whole debate was somewhat unnecessary as he had a reasonable idea he wanted to implement. But when I read Exodus chapter 28, trying to read it from God's perspective, I was able to see that there *are* times when it's important to do things that will give people dignity and honor for the work they have been called to do.

Here's what God asked Moses to do for his brother Aaron, and Aaron's sons, all of whom God had called to become priests in the tabernacle that they were building:

"Make sacred garments for your brother Aaron to give him dignity and honor. Tell all the skilled men to whom I have given wisdom in such matters that they are to make garments for Aaron, for his consecration, so he may serve me as priest" (Exodus 28:2-3).

Then God described in great detail what the robes and turbans and undergarments should look like.

I don't know what you might think about this idea today, whether or not pastors or priests should wear elaborate robes. But the passage indicates to me that there are times when God asks us to give dignity and honor to the people around us, sometimes in very

Give Dignity & Honor To Those Serving With You

specific ways, and that God wants us to listen —and do—what He tells us to do.

I was reading this passage when I was getting ready to launch our newly redesigned website for *The Ranch*. As I tried to think what God might want me to do for those who helped me with the project, I felt He wanted me to have a special online prayer and dedication service for them. So I set a date and time, and invited about a dozen people to join me in the chat room.

We had someone from Latvia who had helped redesign the website. We had someone from Denmark who built the software on which the whole system runs. We had someone from Colorado who helps with our prayer ministry and answering emails. We had someone from North Carolina who serves on our board.

I had sent each of them a small bottle of oil, based on a passage we're going to look at next week, but touched on in this passage, so that I could pray for them, anointing and consecrating them for their work of service to God.

I was very hesitant at first, because in some ways, it seemed—well—just very weird to do this over the Internet! I thought it would be hard to really give them dignity and honor like this. But I've also prayed for enough people over the Internet by now to know that prayer has no boundaries.

So as I prayed for each person, I asked them to put some oil on their finger and touch it to their forehead as I typed out my prayers on my keyboard. I later heard back from several of those who came who said that as we prayed together, they had completely broken down in tears, weeping at this special expression of appreciation for their work of service to God.

What about those who work with you? Is there a way that God might want you to give them dignity and honor? I believe that if you'll ask God, He'll answer you. He may not tell you to put a robe on them. But whatever He tells you, when you do it, God will touch people through it.

Lesson 29

ANOINT, ORDAIN, AND CONSECRATE THOSE SERVING

Scripture Reading: Exodus 28:41-29:35

What can we do for the people who work with us to dedicate them—and their gifts and talents—to the Lord? One thing to consider is "anointing" them with oil.

It seems like an ancient practice, anointing people with oil. But one of the most dramatic experiences of my life was an ordination service where I truly felt God Himself was calling me into His service. He used the hands of a pastor to anoint my head with oil, ordaining and consecrating me for the work God had called me to do.

Throughout the Bible, God anointed some of His most powerful leaders with oil for their work of service to Him, like King David, King Saul, and in the passage we're looking at today, the priest Aaron and his sons:

"After you put these clothes on your brother Aaron

and his sons, anoint and ordain them. Consecrate them so they may serve me as priests" (Exodus 28:41).

I happened to be in Israel when I read some of these passages about anointing people with oil. It's one thing to read these passages at home. It's another thing entirely to be standing on the spots where these things took place. At one point, I was amazed to think that I was standing at the tomb of Samuel the prophet, the one who walked the very same hills I was walking on when he sought out young David to anoint him as king.

These were real people who had done these things, who lived in real places that still exist today. I wondered what it would be like if God were to send someone to anoint me, right there in Israel, for the work He had called me to do. I had recently quit my job to go into full-time ministry and wondered if God could consecrate me in this specific way, too. So I began to pray that God would send someone. I couldn't believe He did it when it happened the very next day!

I ran into a tour group and began talking to a pastor and his wife. They kept asking me questions about how I had quit my job and gone into ministry. I really didn't want to stand around and chit-chat—I was waiting for God to show up! But as we talked, the pastor asked if I had ever anointed people with oil when I prayed for the sick, as he had found that to be very effective.

I couldn't believe it! I hadn't told him anything about my prayer the day before that God would send someone to anoint me with oil. Yet here was a man standing in front of me who regularly anointed people with oil. I hesitantly asked him if he would pray for me, too, anointing me with oil for the work that God had called me to do. He said he would, and at the next stop on the tour, he'd pick up a bottle of oil at one of the local shops to do it.

So I walked with their group from the Temple Mount, down the Way of the Cross, where Jesus carried his cross to his crucifixion. The tour stopped at the church that now houses the crucifixion site. We bought a little bottle of oil, and went into the church to pray.

There, about 20 feet from the foot of the cross which marks the spot where Jesus is said to have died, this man and his wife prayed for me. They anointed me with oil for the work of service God had called me to do. Their prayers were accompanied—at 1:00 sharp—by the loud ringing of church bells overhead, the sounds of a tour group singing hymns, and as sights and smells of burning incense wafted through the room.

I was overwhelmed by the way God had answered my prayers. I'll never look at an anointing service as just an ancient ritual again. It is a powerful means by which God can ordain and consecrate us for our work of service to Him.

God used an earthly man to anoint, ordain and consecrate me for my work, and has since used me to do the same for others. Perhaps God wants to touch those around you in a similar way, praying for them that they would use their gifts and talents to bear much fruit for Him.

Lesson 30

MULTIPLY FREEDOM BY INVOLVING OTHERS

Scripture Reading: Exodus 18:17-19

What could you do to lighten the load of all that God wants you to do? As a summary of the last nine lessons, here's a short list of some of the things God had Moses do to lighten his load. These things not only lightened his load, but they allowed God to accomplish through Moses all that God wanted to do. Maybe they could help you to accomplish more, too.

1) Delegate. Jethro helped Moses to see that Moses would only wear himself out unless he involved others in the work.
2) Write it down. God helped Moses to write down what he had already learned from God, and would need to know in the future, so that Moses could share this wisdom with others.
3) Trust God's timing. God showed Moses a huge vision for what He want-

ed to do through Moses, but God also told him that it wouldn't happen overnight, but rather, little by little.
4) Listen for God's specific instructions. God spoke in specific detail about how God wanted the people to do the work —and Moses listened.
5) Give dignity and honor to those serving with you. God showed Moses not only specific ways to involve others, but also how to give them dignity and honor for their work.

By putting a system in place, Moses was able to multiply the number of people who could experience the freedom God had in mind for them, including us today who still benefit from those words. Moses still had meaningful work to do, but he was relieved from having to do it all himself.

As I wrote this lesson, I had just returned from a missions trip to Africa. My wife and I had been wanting to do something to help the people of Africa in some way, but we had no idea what to do. The problems facing that continent are overwhelming. But after voicing our desire to each other and to God, God showed us a way that we cold help. He invited us to join a missions trip to Swaziland to plant hundreds of small vegetable gardens in people's backyards.

The project was simple enough in theory, but took a huge amount of planning and effort to make it work in practice. We certainly couldn't have done it alone. Thankfully, we didn't have to.

God raised up people to help in dozens of ways: donors who funded the trip, drivers who helped us get through the mountains, pastors who went ahead of us to prepare the people for what we were going to do, translators who helped us interact with the local people, administrators who handled the logistics for our team, and secretaries who arranged hundreds of details during the week.

If we had tried to do this alone, the five of us who went from Streator might have planted five or ten gardens the whole week. But, by involving others, God was able to use our team of 80 volunteers, working alongside the beautiful people of Swaziland, to plant and distribute over 8,000 of these small vegetable gardens. Over the past few years, thousands of volunteers, on dozens of similar trips, have been able to plant and distribute hundreds of thousands of these life-giving gardens.

I often think that I'm the one that has to accomplish the whole vision that God puts on my heart. While I'm willing to do the work, I get overwhelmed because there's too much work to do. The truth is there *is* too much work to do—at least for one person. But by involving others, we can finish the work together.

If you feel overwhelmed by the visions that God has put on your heart, remember that Moses needed help, too. Remember Jethro's words to Moses:

> *"What you are doing is not good. You and these people who come to you will only wear yourselves out. The work is too heavy for you; you cannot handle it alone. Listen now to me and I will give you some advice, and may God be with you..." (Exodus 18:17b-19a).*

Moses took Jethro's advice by involving others—and God *was* with him. May God be with you, too.

Lesson 31

God Wants To Meet With Us And Speak To Us

Scripture Reading: Exodus 29:36-46

There's nothing better than to be with someone you love, spending an extended period of time with them, day and night. Over the next ten lessons we're going to focus on worshiping God, and what it feels to be in love with, and spend extended time with Him.

Since I first read about prayer and fasting in the Bible, I've tried it for various amounts of time. Why would I want to give up food to pray for a day, or five days, or ten, twenty or forty days? It's not because I like giving up food. I don't! But I love being with God. I've found that when I empty myself of the things of the world, it makes more room in my life to be filled with the things of God.

In Exodus 29:38-56, God told the Israelites to make a sacrifice to Him every day in the morning, and every day in the evening at the entrance to the Tent of Meeting. There He would meet with them, and speak to them.

> *"This is what you are to offer on the altar regularly each day: two lambs a year old. Offer one in the morning and the other at twilight....a pleasing aroma, an offering made to the LORD by fire. For the generations to come this burnt offering is to be made regularly at the entrance to the Tent of Meeting before the LORD. There I will meet you and speak to you; there also I will meet with the Israelites, and the place will be consecrated by my glory" (Exodus 29:38-39, 41b-43).*

This is why God set the Israelites free, so He could meet with them and speak to them. It's the same reason He set you and me free, so He could meet with us and speak to us.

Thankfully, we don't have to wait till Sunday, or any special time of the year. We can meet with God every morning and every evening. And God *wants* to meet with us, live with us and speak to us.

When I first became a Christian, I began a habit of setting aside time every morning and every evening to spend time with God. I would wake up early, take my Bible and a journal, and spend time with God before I went to work. Then in the evenings, I would take time to read more from the Bible, or another Christian book—something that would focus my thoughts on Him again at night.

I've found that whenever I've regularly done this over the years, it has helped me to sandwich in my day, between waking up and going to bed. I'll get my marching orders in the morning, then recap the day again in the evening. It can be hard to keep this schedule, and there are times when I haven't kept it up. But reading this passage has reminded me again of the value setting aside time twice a day to intentionally be with God.

A number of godly men and women over the years have made this a regular practice in their lives. Saints of the past, and saints of today, have written daily devotionals for this purpose with titles like Charles Spurgeon's *Morning and Evening,* or Joyce Meyers' *Starting Your Day Right: Devotions for Each Morning of the Year* and *Ending Your Day Right: Devotions for Every Evening of the Year.* You can sign up at various websites on the Internet, like www.crosswalk.com, and receive a devotional twice a day by email.

It's not always easy to carve out time to spend time with God. But it's so worth it. Sacrificing this way for God is like a lucky honeymoon couple going to Hawaii for a week. They don't get in the plane because they want to sit in a cramped seat for hours on end. They do it because when they get there, they'll get to spend uninterrupted time with their beloved, day and night.

Take time today, and every day—even twice a day—to get away with your Beloved. He wants to meet with you and speak with you.

Lesson 32

MAKE A PLACE TO MEET WITH GOD TWICE A DAY

Scripture Reading: Exodus 30:1-16

Last time we looked at making a time to meet with God twice a day. Today we'll look at making a place to meet with God twice a day, a place where we can truly "worship" Him.

In Exodus 30, God asked Aaron to build an altar for burning incense. This was to be a fragrant offering to God, twice a day:

> *"Make an altar of acacia wood for burning incense. ... Aaron must burn fragrant incense on the altar every morning when he tends the lamps. He must burn incense again when he lights the lamps at twilight so incense will burn regularly before the LORD for the generations to come" (Exodus 30:1,7-8).*

I know I'm not Aaron, but as I read this passage, I was trying to think of a way that I could do something similar every morning and every evening as part of my own quiet time with God.

Although my piano's not made of acacia wood, I decided that I could use it as an altar. This wasn't to be a thing that I could worship, but a place where I could worship, a place where I could send up my own fragrant offering to the Lord. As Aaron tended the lamps every morning and every evening, I thought I could light a candle there by my piano, too. Then as I would play the piano, or sing a song, or put my Bible on the front of the piano and read some scripture from it, I would have a visual reminder that these moments were dedicated to God.

After doing this for several weeks, I found out that lighting the candle reminded me to focus on Him, making this a special time of personal worship. This wasn't to be a time to ask God for things, but a time to make a fragrant offering of my life to Him, serving Him, pleasing Him and spending time with Him.

The lit candle reminded me that my quiet time isn't just a time to be alone. *It's a time to be with God.*

It's amazing how that simple act of lighting the candle twice a day, and playing a song, let me know if I had truly spent time with God during the day. I would sometimes think, "Oh, yeah, I read my Bible this morning," or "I thought about God as I got out of bed," or "I prayed about something as I jumped in the car." The candle helped me to focus not just on thinking "about" God, but being "with" God.

Do you have a place where you can go to worship God? A quiet spot in your house, or somewhere else, where you can meet with Him, twice a day? My wife, Lana, put a chair in a closet several years ago and goes in there from time to time when she needs an extra special time with God. Although there's barely enough room for her feet in the closet, it's enough room for her to cozy up with her Bible and journal and focus solely on Him.

Some of my friends have a special desk where they sit on a straight back chair to help keep them awake and focused. Others sit at their kitchen table, or on their front porch when the weather's nice, or jump in their truck with the motor turned off. Some keep a Bible and notepad by their bed so they can spend time with God the first and last thing every day.

One of the best places I've found in my busy house is in the bathtub! With the bathroom fan running and the curtain pulled, this drowns out many of the other sounds and distractions in the house. I've accidentally baptized a couple of Bibles doing this. But the time with God is awesome!

If you don't already have a place, consider finding one where you can spend time with God every morning and every evening. Try several places! This is not only to help you form a lifelong habit of a daily quiet time with God, but can also help you experience changes in your life, and your relationship with Him, as a result of the time you spend together each day.

Lesson 33

CLEANSE AND CONSECRATE YOURSELF FOR WORSHIP

Scripture Reading: Exodus 30:17-38

Today I'd like to talk about why we sometimes aren't able to fully come into worship. We want to worship God, but we're held back by something.

Exodus 30 gives us a clue about one of the things that can hold us back—and how to get past it. There was something that Aaron and his sons were to do every time they came into the place of worship, and something that would happen if they didn't:

> *"Then the LORD said to Moses, 'Make a bronze basin, with its bronze stand, for washing. Place it between the Tent of Meeting and the altar, and put water in it. Aaron and his sons are to wash their hands and feet with water from it. Whenever they enter the Tent of Meeting, they shall wash with water so that they will not die'" (Exodus 30:18-20a).*

They were to wash their hands and feet in water from a bronze basin whenever they entered the place of worship. If they didn't, they'd die! It seems like God was pretty serious about getting clean before coming into His presence!

Sometimes we get pretty lax about coming into the presence of God. I know I do. I love to be able to come to God *Just As I Am,* like the famous song that's sung at Billy Graham crusades. But this passage is a reminder to me that if I'm ever finding it hard to fully enter into worship, it would be good to look and see if there's anything in my life that might need cleansing—not physically with water, but inwardly in my heart or life.

I've had guys share with me that they're struggling in a relationship with their wife. I'll sometimes ask them if there's anything they haven't told their wife, anything that they might have done to sin against her. Oftentimes, they'll say, "Yes." It's no surprise then that they find their relationship with their wife has cooled off. Who wants to be around someone else when they've sinned against them and haven't confessed it?

One man told me he was struggling with

intimacy with his wife. Then he also told me he was struggling with homosexual pornography. I asked him if he had ever talked to his wife about this struggle. "Of course not!" he answered, "it would hurt her too much if I told her."

I told him, "Buddy, it's hurting her too much now, every day, and it's playing out in every part of your relationship with her. It's not going to hurt her more by telling her, it's going to finally help you, and her, start to get the healing you both need." I'm fully aware that there are better and worse times for confessing these things, and there are better and worse ways to communicate the truth. But ultimately, it is the truth that will set us free.

It's similar in our relationships with God. Sometimes we have sin in our lives, sins against Him, and we don't really feel like spending time with Him. We don't feel like worshiping Him. But if we would confess our sins to God, and come clean to Him, we'd be much more eager to come into His presence.

Confession is critical, especially to God. It shows God, or the other person, that you really do care about your relationship with them. Rather than driving them away, it usually draws them closer to you.

If there's anything on your heart that you want to confess to God, maybe you'd like to take some time right now to get things right with Him again. It might only take 30 seconds after you finish reading this note to just talk to Him and say, "I'm sorry for what I've done. I pray that You'd forgive me." It might take a few hours or days. But whatever it takes, do it. Come clean. The cleansing you'll feel afterwards can make the worship you experience later all the more sweet.

And here's an encouraging promise from God's Word:

"If we confess our sins, he is faithful and just and will forgive us our sins and purify us from all unrighteousness" (1 John 1:19).

Lesson 34

God Chooses And Equips People To Do His Work

Scripture Reading: Exodus 31:1-11

If you feel like you're not very gifted or skilled, or if you wonder if God's going to use you in any special way, today's lesson is for you. God *does* choose and equip people to do His work.

In the last few chapters of Exodus, God has gone into considerable detail telling Moses how to make all kinds of things for the place of worship: the tapestries, altar, utensils, incense and oils. Now God tells Moses how it would all get done: God had chosen and equipped people to do His work:

"Then the LORD said to Moses, 'See, I have chosen Bezalel...and I have filled him with the Spirit of God, with skill, ability and knowledge in all kinds of crafts—to make artistic designs for work in gold, silver and bronze, to cut and set stones, to work in wood, and to engage in all kinds of craftsmanship. Moreover, I have appointed Oholiab...to

help him. Also I have given skill to all the craftsmen to make everything I have commanded you' " (Exodus 31:1-6).

What was the very first thing with which God had filled Bezalel? The Spirit of God. It's encouraging to me to know that when God calls us to do something, He will, first and foremost, fill us with His Spirit so we can do it.

I remember praying for a man on the night he gave his life to the Lord. As we talked, he told me he had really wanted to read his Bible, but in the 50+ years he had been alive, he had never been able to do it. So I prayed with him: "Lord, fill him with Your Spirit so that he can do the things he wants to do."

I left my Bible with him and the next day he started reading it. Then he bought his own Bible and kept reading it. Within a few weeks, he had finished the New Testament, so he went back to the Old Testament and read it, too. Then he started reading the whole thing all over again, and began passing out Bibles to all his friends. Now he's a pastor of a church!

If you feel like you're not able to do what God's called you to do, ask Him again: "Father, fill me with Your Spirit so I can do the things You want me to do."

But God didn't stop there with Bezalel. God also filled him with "skill, ability and knowledge in all kinds of crafts." God also said He'd send yet another man, Oholiab, to help Bezelel, along with many other people to help them both. God equipped all of them with various skills, abilities and knowledge to do His work.

Asking God to equip you isn't a "magical" prayer. I've anointed my hands with oil and prayed that God would help me to play the piano better. After washing off my hands, I sat down to play again—and it sounded just like it did before! But over time, God has answered that prayer by giving me more and more opportunities to play and lead worship and develop my skills.

Now this is just a guess on my part, but where do you think all those Israelites got their skills, abilities and knowledge to do all kinds of intricate work with gold, silver and bronze? Remember that they had just been slaves in Egypt, working for kings who were later buried in those incredible pyramids. Have you ever seen the coffins or other things they've brought out of Egypt, like King Tut's headpiece, or the other intricate carvings found in his tomb? Who worked on all that stuff? It's probably fair to say that a number of the slaves helped to carry out the details of that elaborate work.

I wonder if the Israelites might have felt that all those years were wasted, making images of someone else's gods. But now, God was calling them to use their gifts and skills for Him, to make a place of worship that far surpassed anything they had ever done before.

Keep praying that God will fill you with His Spirit, giving you skills, abilities and knowledge that you can ultimately use for Him.

Lesson 35

OBSERVE THE SABBATH

Scripture Reading: Exodus 31:12-18

How would it feel if your boss came to you this week and said, "Why don't you take a day off this week. It's no problem. You've worked hard, just go home and get some rest." I think that would feel great!

The truth is, that's what God says to us every week.

Even when God gives us a huge task to do, He still wants us to be sure to take a break every seven days, just like He wanted Moses and the Israelites to take a break when they had a huge task before them.

In the chapters leading up to Exodus 31, God has laid out in detail all the work that the Israelites would need to do to build their house of worship. The work would take many months to complete. But at the end of everything God called them to do, God closed with these words:

"For six days, work is to be done, but the seventh day is a Sabbath of rest, holy to the LORD. Whoever does any work on the Sabbath day must be put to death. The Israelites are to observe the Sabbath, celebrating it for the generations to come as a lasting covenant. It will be a sign between me and the Israelites forever, for in six days the LORD made the heavens and the earth, and on the seventh day he abstained from work and rested" (Exodus 31:15-18).

God Himself took a break at the end of a long, hard week of creating the universe, and we've been on a seven-day calendar ever since. Like so many of God's laws, the penalty of death wasn't meant to be mean, but to emphasize just how critical this law would be to our own well-being. God knows how we're wired. He's the One who wired us! He knows that we need a rest every seven days, and He's thrilled to give it to us.

I grew up on a farm in Illinois, and my Dad worked as hard as anyone I knew. But not on Sunday. It didn't matter if there was still work to be done or not, or whether it was raining or sunny, Dad took off—and we did, too. It was great! (As a side note: the Sabbath for Jews is from sunset on Friday through sunset on Saturday, whereas the early Christians began to celebrate the Sabbath on Sunday, the "Lord's Day," which is the day Jesus rose from the dead.)

One Sunday night, my wife Lana began to make a big lasagna dinner for some guests we were having over for dinner on Monday night. I didn't think it was a very good way for her to spend her "day off." But when we were talking about it with a friend a few weeks later, our friend asked Lana if making the lasagna dinner brought "rest to her soul." Lana said it really did, because she was able to enjoy the whole process of making the dinner while I watched the kids.

For Lana, making that lasagna dinner was truly relaxing and restful. I had to wonder if Jesus wasn't smiling at me and my legalistic view of the Sabbath. The religious leaders of Jesus' day looked at what He was doing as breaking the Sabbath rules, too, like healing others, or allowing His disciples to gather food from the fields (Matthew 12:1-14). But rather than breaking the law, Jesus was revealing the heart of the law, a law which was designed to bring true "rest to our souls," a kind of rest which Jesus still offers to all who come to Him as well:

> *"Come to me, all you who are weary and burdened, and I will give you rest. Take my yoke upon you and learn from me, for I am gentle and humble in heart, and you will find rest for your souls. For my yoke is easy and my burden is light"* (Matthew 11:28-30).

What about you? What would you do this week that would truly bring rest to your soul? God may be eagerly waiting and hoping you'll do that very thing, too!

Lesson 36

People Will Worship, But What?

Scripture Reading: Exodus 32:1-6

As human beings, we want to worship something. We desire to worship, we're wired to worship, and we will worship. But what will we worship?

One of my missionary friends says that his definition of missions is to help people turn away from worshiping anything that was pulling them away from God, so that they could worship the One True God. It isn't a matter of whether or not people will worship, but a matter of who or what they will worship.

Exodus 32 gives us one of the clearest pictures of this truth in the Bible.

While Moses was spending forty days and nights in the presence of God, getting the detailed plans for what God wanted them to do next, the Israelites were growing impatient down at the bottom of the mountain. They went to Moses' right-hand man and brother, Aaron, saying,

> *"Come, make us gods who will go before us. As for this fellow Moses who brought us up out of Egypt, we don't know what has happened to him" (Exodus 32:1b).*

Now Aaron, having seen all the great signs and wonders that God had just finished doing for the people, should have naturally said something like this: "Didn't you see that pillar of fire? That cloud of smoke? Those Egyptians smashed by the waves of the sea? What are you thinking?" But that's not what Aaron said. He said:

> *" 'Take off the gold earrings that your wives, your sons and your daughters are wearing, and bring them to me.' So all the people took off their earrings and brought them to Aaron. He took what they handed him and made it into an idol cast in the shape of a calf, fashioning it with a tool. Then they said, 'These are your gods, O Israel, who brought you up out of Egypt.' ... Afterward they sat down to eat and drink and got up to indulge in revelry" (Exodus 32:2-4, 6b).*

People Will Worship, But What?

The people grew impatient waiting for what God had in mind for them. God knew it was in their hearts to shape and fashion things out of gold. He had a blueprint in mind for them that was about to blow them away with the magnificence and awe of it, and would inspire in their hearts for impassioned worship. But instead, they chose to put their God-given skills to use in ways that took them further from God, instead of drawing them closer to Him.

I had a friend who told me about her 32-year old daughter who had decided to pursue a lesbian relationship. My friend asked me how she could continue to show love and acceptance to her daughter, without approving of the relationship. She especially wondered how she could possibly ask her daughter to give up this relationship, when it seemed like this was the first time her daughter had been happy in her entire life. What could I say?

I told her: "Your daughter may be really happy for the first time in her life. It sounds like she's found someone who loves and accepts her. There's nothing wrong with a loving and accepting friendship—we all need those. But it's the sexualization of that friendship that isn't what God wants for her. If she thinks what she has now is good, imagine what God has in store for her! God says He can do immeasurably more than all we can ask or imagine."

I know in my own life I was happy, having fun, and thought I was doing fine—until I put my faith in Christ. But when I started reading the Bible, I saw that God had more in store for me. What I was doing would never bring me to that point, and would probably destroy me, like it eventually destroyed the Israelites. Many of them died as a result.

Looking back on my life, the happiness I experienced then pales in comparison to what God has given me now. I was trying to meet my valid needs, but in invalid ways.

We're all going to worship something. It's a valid need we all have. But only by worshiping the One True God can we truly satisfy that need, for our benefit, and for His.

Lesson 37

WE CAN TURN PEOPLE BACK WHEN THEY TURN AWAY

Scripture Reading: Exodus 32:7-14

Have you ever tried to help someone out with their life, only to see them turn away from God? You wonder if they'll ever turn back around? You think to yourself, "Man, I could really help that person if they would just let me."

I want to encourage you that all is not lost when our friends, family, or co-workers turn away from God. Even though they may be quick to turn away from God, we can turn them back. We have the power of the Living God in our lives to help turn their lives around.

Take encouragement from what happened to Moses in Exodus chapter 32. When God and Moses finished talking on the mountain, God gave Moses a heads-up about what was going on back at camp. God said:

"Go down, because your people, whom you brought

up out of Egypt, have become corrupt. They have been quick to turn away from what I commanded them and have made themselves an idol cast in the shape of a calf. They have bowed down to it and sacrificed to it and have said, 'These are your gods, O Israel, who brought you up out of Egypt' " *(Exodus 32:8-9).*

If you've followed the story of these people up to this point, what do you think you would do with them now? They've just seen miracle after miracle after miracle of God working in their lives. They've just been set free from 400 years of bondage in slavery. Yet here they are, a short time later, and again, they're turning their back on God.

Here's what God thought of doing at this point:

"I have seen these people," the LORD said to Moses, "and they are a stiff-necked people. Now leave me alone so that my anger may burn against them and that I may destroy them. Then I will make you into a great nation" (Exodus 32:10).

Moses may have felt the exact same thing. But when Moses heard what God was about to do, something clicked within Moses. He said, in effect, "No, God, don't do it!"

Moses didn't plead the innocence of the people, like we might try to do regarding our friends, saying, "It's just a calf, they'll turn back. Let 'em go, it's no big deal." Moses didn't try to argue on the people's behalf based on their merit, but based on God's promises:

> *"O LORD," he said, "why should your anger burn against your people, whom you brought out of Egypt with great power and a mighty hand? Why should the Egyptians say, 'It was with evil intent that he brought them out, to kill them in the mountains and to wipe them off the face of the earth'? Turn from your fierce anger; relent and do not bring disaster on your people. Remember your servants Abraham, Isaac and Israel, to whom you swore by your own self: 'I will make your descendants as numerous as the stars in the sky and I will give your descendants all this land I promised them, and it will be their inheritance forever.'" Then the LORD relented and did not bring on his people the disaster he had threatened (Exodus 32:8-14).*

Something similar happened back in Genesis chapter 6 when God threatened to destroy the earth with a flood. But on account of Noah, God gave humanity another chance.

While it's true that people can be quick to turn away from God, it's also true that we can turn them back. We have the power of the Living God with us to help turn their lives around.

We can stand in the gap for them. We can pray for them. We can listen to them, speak the truth to them, and show love to them. Remember that God is *"not wanting anyone to perish, but everyone to come to repentance" (2 Peter 3:9b).*

Call out to God on their behalf, saying, "God, please spare my daughter from the bad decisions she's made. Spare my son, my boss, my mother, my father, my brother, my friend. Have mercy on them Lord, not because of their goodness, but because of Yours. In Jesus' name, Amen."

Lesson 38

WE MUST DEAL WITH SIN WITH A HEART LIKE JESUS

Scripture Reading: Exodus 32:15-35

If we want to help set others free from sin, at some point we must deal with their sin. But the way we deal with it makes all the difference in the world.

We can learn a lesson from the way Moses dealt with the sin of his people when they created a golden calf and began to worship it.

Moses was hot with anger at their sin, and God called Moses to administer justice to the people. But even in Moses' righteous anger, he only took things as far as God told him to —and no further. Even more important, he showed his true heart for God and for the people, by offering his own life as a willing sacrifice in their place.

Take a look at what Moses said the day after he had to administer God's justice to the people:

"The next day Moses said to the people, 'You have

committed a great sin. But now I will go up to the LORD; perhaps I can make atonement for your sin.' So Moses went back to the LORD and said, 'Oh, what a great sin these people have committed! They have made themselves gods of gold. But now, please forgive their sin—but if not, then blot me out of the book you have written' " (Exodus 32:31-32).

Moses had done what God had told him to do, but his words reveal the heart from which he had done it. He admitted that the people had sinned, not glossing over it, not trying to minimize it, but acknowledging that it was great indeed. But he also called on God to forgive their sin, adding that if God wouldn't forgive them, then to please blot his own name out of God's book.

Moses was able to effectively execute justice because he was also willing to take the same punishment upon himself as what might have come to those who had sinned. He didn't come against them as one who was merely outraged by their actions, even though he *was* outraged. He came to them as one who was also willing to stand in the gap for them.

Doesn't that sound like someone else in the Bible? It sounds to me like Jesus.

It sounds exactly like what Jesus did for us when he willingly died on the cross. He hadn't done anything wrong. In fact, He had done everything right. But because of His great love for us, He was willing to take upon Himself the punishment that we rightfully deserved for our sin.

This is the kind of heart that God wants us to have when He calls us to deal with other people's sin: a heart full of love. I've been in situations where I haven't had this kind of heart. But I've known that I've needed to do whatever it took to get this kind of heart before I would be able to effectively confront the sin in another person's life.

Even though we can't die in the place of others, as Jesus did, we can have hearts that are willing to do so. We can have the same kind of heart that Jesus had. We can walk with people through their struggles. We can talk with them as they try to find their way out. We can listen to them as they anguish over the very real, and sometimes very precious things they may need to leave behind in order to get free. We can ask God's forgiveness for them, even when they repeatedly make mistakes on their road to recovery.

The Bible says that Jesus is the only one who can condemn any of us, but instead of condemning us, He's sitting at the right hand of God, praying for us (see Romans 8:34).

That's the kind of heart God wants us to have for others when we deal with their sin. A heart that can feel the pain that God feels when people sin, but a heart that is also willing to stand in the gap for them when they do. God wants us to deal with sin from a heart full of love—a heart just like Jesus.

Lesson 39

MEETING WITH GOD

Scripture Reading: Exodus 33:1-17

For me, one of the most encouraging things to read about in the Bible is when people meet with God. It's amazing to me that God not only met with people in the Bible, but that He also wants to meet with us.

One of those biblical meetings occurs in the middle of Exodus chapter 33, which describes how Moses would often meet with God.

> *"Now Moses used to take a tent and pitch it outside the camp some distance away, calling it the 'tent of meeting.' Anyone inquiring of the LORD would go to the tent of meeting outside the camp. And whenever Moses went out to the tent, all the people rose and stood at the entrances to their tents, watching Moses until he entered the tent. As Moses went into the tent, the pillar of cloud would come down and stay at the entrance, while the LORD*

spoke with Moses. Whenever the people saw the pillar of cloud standing at the entrance to the tent, they all stood and worshiped, each at the entrance to his tent. The LORD would speak to Moses face to face, as a man speaks with his friend. Then Moses would return to the camp, but his young aide Joshua son of Nun did not leave the tent" (Exodus 33:7-11).

This passage is tucked in the midst of a very difficult time in the life of the Israelites. God was really angry with them for what they had just done, by turning away from Him. After dealing with their sin, God told them to go ahead of Him into the promised land. Then God added, *"But I will not go with you, because you are a stiff-necked people and I might destroy you on the way"* (Exodus 33:3b).

The people were distressed to hear this. So Moses did again what was apparently something he had been doing already on a regular basis. He went out to meet with God in the "tent of meeting."

I think many of us go through times when we feel like God is really close to us, then go through other times when we feel He is far from us. There are many reasons for this kind of ebb and flow in our relationship with God. But I know for me, if God seems distant, I want to make sure it isn't because I have become "stiff-necked," like God described had happened to the people in this passage. I want to make sure my neck is well-lubricated, and fully turned towards Him.

I remember an author who described a time in his own life when he was feeling empty in the things he was doing for God. He realized that he was using his own skills and abilities more and more to serve God, but relying on God less and less. In order to regain His full reliance on God to do what God had called him to do, he realized he needed to turn back to God again in a personal relationship that was real and vibrant.

As part of his personal renewal, he made a commitment to himself to write out his dialog with God daily, filling at least one page of a notebook per day. By intentionally carving out time to be with God again, he was able to recapture the joy and fullness of serving Him.

We don't have to deliberately sin to feel like God is distant. But sometimes through our busy-ness, laziness, or plain neglect, we can find ourselves farther and farther from the one true relationship that matters most: our relationship with God.

God wants to meet with us. And when we put our faith in Christ, God promises to send His Holy Spirit to not only meet with us, but to live within us (see Romans 8:11), and to speak with us, too:

> *"But when he, the Spirit of truth, comes, he will guide you into all truth. He will not speak on his own; he will speak only what he hears, and he will tell you what is yet to come" (John 16:13).*

God wants to meet with you, too. Take time to meet with Him today.

Lesson 40

WE'RE SET FREE TO WORSHIP

Scripture Reading: Exodus 33:11

We've reached lesson 40 of this 50 lesson study of the book of Exodus. Before we head into the final 10 lessons of this study, I'd like to remind you of the purpose of "the Exodus," of getting free, in the first place.

God sets us free so we can worship Him. We don't have to wait till we die and go to heaven to be in the presence of God. We don't have to wait till we get to the end of some spiritual journey to be with Him. We don't even have to wait one more minute.

We can worship God in our hearts right now. We can spend time in His presence, commune with Him, at any given moment.

There's a little passage tucked in Exodus 33 that reminds me of this. The Bible says that when Moses would want to spend time with God, he would go to the "Tent of Meeting," and God would meet with him there. But then the Bible adds these words:

> *"Then Moses would return to the camp, but his young aide Joshua son of Nun did not leave the tent" (Exodus 33:11b).*

I try to picture what it would be like to be a young aide to Moses, the great deliverer of the people of Israel. What would it be like to walk beside him into the tent of meeting, and watch him as the Lord would, *"speak to Moses face to face, as a man speaks to his friend" (Exodus 33:11a)?*

I think it would be awesome! Apparently, so did Joshua. Since Moses was the leader of the nation, he had to then go back to the camp to deal with the issues of the day. But not Joshua. Joshua stayed. He wasn't about to leave that tent. He was going to stay right there in the presence of God.

Although they hadn't reached the promised land yet, they could still spend time in the presence of God. Although they hadn't resolved all of the problems and struggles of life, they could still worship Him. Although they were still in the midst of one of the worst struggles of their nation, this didn't deter Joshua from spending time in the "tent of meeting." Rather than deterring the people, it probably drove them even deeper into the presence of the Living God.

Sometimes we think that we have to reach a certain place in our freedom before we can fully worship God. We think that we have to get free of a particular sin, or be fully restored from a broken relationship. Or we wonder if we might never really be able to worship God here on this earth, but will only get to *truly* enter His presence when we die.

But this passage in Exodus, as well as many others throughout the Bible, encourage me that we can, at any moment, step into the presence of God. Sure, it's a lot easier to step into His presence when we're not weighted down with sin and strife and struggle. That's why God wants us so desperately to throw off anything that might entangle us.

And yet, sometimes, it's the very act of coming into His presence that helps us to finally surrender our grip on those things that are holding us back, letting God Himself take the weights off of our shoulders. As Joshua would later find out, when Moses died and

Joshua had to take over the leadership of the entire nation, those regular moments in the presence of God would prove invaluable to his own effectiveness as a leader.

Whether there's peace all around you, or strife swirling out of control, I'd like to encourage you to step into God's presence sometime today, even right now if you can. Like Joshua, maybe you can just stay there and linger awhile with God, like a honeymoon couple enjoying some intimate moments together.

Worshiping God is one of the most glorious, life-giving, and life producing acts in which we can engage. It's the reason God set us free in the first place. Why not take a little time to just step into his presence today?

Lesson 41

Ask God To Show You His Glory

Scripture Reading: Exodus 33:18-23

I'd like you to listen in to a conversation that took place several thousand years ago between God and Moses. In this conversation, you'll learn something about what it's like to have an intimate relationship with God, and what you can do to take that relationship even deeper.

The conversation takes place in chapter 33 of the book of Exodus. Moses has just been pleading with God to come with him on the next leg of his journey.

> *The LORD replied, "My Presence will go with you, and I will give you rest." Then Moses said to him, "If your Presence does not go with us, do not send us up from here. How will anyone know that you are pleased with me and with your people unless you go with us? What else will distinguish me and your people from all the other people on the face of the earth?"*

> *And the LORD said to Moses, "I will do the very thing you have asked, because I am pleased with you and I know you by name."*
> *Then Moses said, "Now show me your glory."*
> *And the LORD said, "I will cause all my goodness to pass in front of you, and I will proclaim my name, the LORD, in your presence" (Exodus 33:14-19a).*

What's amazing to me about this conversation is that throughout this whole journey called "the exodus" from Egypt, Moses has been walking with God, talking with God, and seeing God work in various ways. And yet, here in chapter 33, Moses is still asking to see more and more of God. He says to God, "Now show me your glory."

One of the lessons I get out of this conversation is that no matter how close we are to God, or how close we have been in the past, we can always go deeper with Him. There's always more to learn about Him. There's always more that God wants to reveal to us about Himself, if we're willing to ask.

Maybe this is one of the reasons God makes it possible for us to spend eternity in heaven with Him when we put our faith in

Christ, because it will take that long to get to know Him as deeply as possible.

This idea of spending time with God so that we can get to know Him more is a huge part of what it means to experience His "glory." If you look closely at the conversation, you'll see that God says that He knows Moses by name. He knows who Moses is. He knows what makes Moses tick. He knows his *name.* So when Moses asks to see God's glory, God replies, in essence, "All right, I'll show you *My* name, too. I'll show you more of who I am." God knows Moses, and Moses wants to know God.

In the purest sense, this is at the heart of what it means to be intimate with someone else: to reveal more of yourself to them, and to invite them to reveal more of themselves to you.

In fact, the Hebrew word often used in the Bible to describe the conception of a child is "yada," which means "to know." When the Bible says that "Adam knew Eve," it means that they were so intimate that they conceived a child! (see Genesis 4:1, NKJV) Interestingly, this same word "yada" is used to describe the intimacy that takes place when we worship

God, an intimacy in which we reveal more of ourselves to Him, and He reveals more of Himself to us.

God invites us to be intimate with Him, to worship Him with our entire beings. He wants us to love Him with all of our heart, soul, mind and strength, not rushing through these moments of intimacy, but taking the time to reveal ourselves to each other.

No matter how close to, or far away from God you might feel, take some extra time today to ask Him to reveal more of Himself to you. Ask God to show you His glory.

Lesson 42

ABSORB THE NAME OF THE LORD

Scripture Reading: Exodus 34:1-7

If God wore a name tag, I think today's scripture passage would be on it. A person's name often reveals something about who they are. This was especially true in biblical days. The name "Moses," for instance, meant "drawn out of the water," which describes exactly how he was rescued from the Nile River by one of Pharaoh's daughters.

God's name reveals to us who He is, too. So when Moses says to God in Exodus 34, "show me Your glory," God responds by saying that He would cause His "name" to pass in front of Moses, thus revealing to Moses more about who He is. Here's what God says:

> *"Then the LORD came down in the cloud and stood there with him and proclaimed his name, the LORD. And he passed in front of Moses, pro-*

claiming, 'The LORD, the LORD, the compassionate and gracious God, slow to anger, abounding in love and faithfulness, maintaining love to thousands, and forgiving wickedness, rebellion and sin. Yet he does not leave the guilty unpunished; he punishes the children and their children for the sin of the fathers to the third and fourth generation' " (Exodus 34:5-7).

God's name tag would read something like this: "Hello, my name is... Compassionate. Gracious. Slow to Anger. Abounding in Love and Faithfulness. Forgiving, Yet Just."

To me, it's an Old Testament description of what Christ came to demonstrate for us in the New Testament. The prophet Jeremiah later tells us that God is going to make a new covenant with the people, not one written on tablets of stone, but one that would be written on people's hearts. Not a covenant where the children would have to pay for the sins of their fathers, but one where each person would be called to account for their own sins.

Some people think that God is portrayed in the Old Testament as being easily provoked to anger. But the way I read it, I see God as incredibly compassionate, gracious and slow to anger. If you read the Bible from beginning to end, you'll see a repeating pattern of God drawing people to Himself, then people turning away. God draws them back, then they turn away. He draws them again, then they turn away again. At some point, if God is a "just" God, He must eventually punish sin.

But if God were merely "just," He would have wiped out the entire planet long ago. In fact, way back in Genesis chapter 6, just six chapters into the history of man, God was tempted to do just that because of the wickedness of the people. But God relented, and gave mankind another chance. And another. And another. The fact that any of us are still alive today is a testimony to God's compassion, grace, and ability to be slow to anger. The fact that God sent Jesus to die, so that anyone who would put their faith in Him would be saved from the punishment of death, shows that He is still willing to go to incredible lengths to be forgiving, yet just.

I've heard the difference between justice, mercy and grace described by the different possible reactions of a man who had caught a thief trying to steal a brand new Harley-

Davidson motorcycle from his garage. If the owner grabbed a gun and shot the thief, or escorted him to jail, that would be justice. The thief was stealing his stuff, and stealing is wrong, so justice requires some kind of penalty.

But if the owner said, "I'm just going to let you go and walk out of here now. Even though what you've done is wrong, I'm not going to touch you, just go," that would be mercy.

But if the owner turned around, went back into the house and got the keys to the Harley, came back and handed them to the thief, signed over the title to him, and handed him $100 to put gas in it, that would be grace.

And that's what God has done for us through Christ:

"But God demonstrates his own love for us in this: While we were still sinners, Christ died for us" (Romans 5:8).

Take time to absorb the name of the Lord, realizing how incredibly loving and gracious He is. Then remember to extend that same love and grace to others.

Lesson 43

WORSHIP AND WONDER

Scripture Reading: Exodus 34:8-10

I've had moments in my life where something will happen and I'll think, "Wow, that was the presence of God passing right in front of me."

I don't always sense His presence like this, but when I do, I'm usually taken aback by it, and I'm not quite sure how to react. It's overwhelming, on one hand, to realize that God has just passed by. But it's often such a small thing, on the other hand, that alerts me to His presence, that it makes me stop and think, "Was that really God?"

I love how Moses responds when the presence of God passed by Him in Exodus chapter 34:

"Moses bowed to the ground at once and worshiped. 'O Lord, if I have found favor in your eyes,' he said, 'then let the Lord go with us. Although this is a stiff-necked people, forgive our wickedness and

our sin, and take us as your inheritance.' Then the LORD said: 'I am making a covenant with you. Before all your people I will do wonders never before done in any nation in all the world. The people you live among will see how awesome is the work that I, the LORD, will do for you' " (Exodus 34:8-10).

Moses' response was immediate: he bowed down and worshiped, "at once."

The night before I wrote this lesson, I had one of those moments where I felt God's presence passing by.

All week I had been thinking about an illustration of what grace looks like that I had read twenty years ago in Victor Hugo's book, *Les Miserables*. In the book, a thief takes refuge in the home of a bishop, who was the first person who offered the thief a meal and lodging since his escape from prison. As they prepared for bed that night, the bishop handed the thief a silver candlestick to light his way to his bedroom for the night.

In the middle of the night, the thief's heart became hard again and he took the opportunity to escape while he still could, stealing the silver utensils that they had used for dinner as he left the house. But early the next morning, the police caught the thief and brought him back to the bishop's house. The bishop exclaimed, "Oh, you are back again! I am glad to see you. I gave you the candlesticks, too, which are silver also, and will bring forty francs. Why did you not take them?"

The thief was stunned, as were the police. The bishop added solemnly, "Never forget you have promised me you would use the money to become an honest man," which is exactly what happened.

I remembered that picture of grace from Hugo's book and wanted to share it with others, but didn't know where in my house to find the book I had once read. The night before I was to write this lesson, my 8 year-old son and I were reading from another book, a large collection of short stories, when my son said, "I'd like to just flip through the pages and pick a story with my fingers." He ran his fingers through the 832 page book and opened it. I stared in disbelief at the title of the story in front of my eyes. It was called, *The Good Bishop,* and it gave a short, 3-page summary of this very incident with the candlesticks from Victor Hugo's book, *Les Misérables*.

I felt as if the presence of God had just passed by.

I wanted to bow down and worship. Not just because God had found the story for me that I had been looking for, in a place where I never would have looked for it, but because earlier in the day I was wondering why some of the "big" things I've been praying about have not yet been answered.

I was reminded that God is not just in the big things—and He's not just in the little things. God is in *every* thing.

The next time God passes by, what will your response be? I'm praying that more and more, my response will be like that of Moses, to bow down at once, and worship.

Lesson 44

Our Role And God's Role

Scripture Reading: Exodus 34:11-28

We're going to look in this lesson at something that puzzles a lot of people, including me. Sometimes we wonder how much we have to do for God, and how much He's going to do for us. It's hard to find the balance. The truth is that we both have roles to play. God has things He wants us to do, and then there are things He says He'll do.

A quick look at Exodus chapter 34, verses 10-28, when God made a covenant with the Israelites, shows these two roles. If you take a look at that passage, you'll see that God says there are things He's going to do, and then He says there are things He wants them to do.

Here are a few things that God says He's going to do for them:

– He'll do wonders never before done in any nation of the world (verse 10)

- He'll drive out the nations ahead of them (verse 11)
- He'll enlarge their territory (verse 24)

And here are a few things that God wants them to do:

- Obey what He commands (verse 11)
- Don't make cast idols (verse 17) (I think this was just a reminder about the golden calf, "That was a bad move guys, don't ever do that again, OK?")
- Celebrate the feasts and make sure to rest every seventh day (verses 18 and 21)

I think this is helpful for our own understanding of how we interact with God.

Sometimes we might sit back and mistakenly say, "It's all in Your hands God. I'm not going to do a thing. I'm leaving it all up to You." There are times when it's important to simply pray, and pray, and pray. But prayer is a conversation with God, and oftentimes during those conversations, God tells us things that He wants us to do. In those times, we've got to do our part.

Other times, we might mistakenly think

that we've got to do everything. We think that if we don't do it, it won't get done. We act as if God's not likely to do *anything* for us. We forget that God has a huge role to play in everything we do. In the case of the Israelites, God's role was to do certain things, like performing wonders never before done in any nation of the world, driving out nations before them, and enlarging their territory—little things like that. :)

So there are often these two things going on at the same time: things God will do, and things He wants us to do. We need to trust God to do His part, and we need to do our part to the best of our ability.

There's a final point in this passage that I don't want you to miss. God ends His conversation with Moses with these words:

> *"Then the LORD said to Moses, 'Write down these words, for in accordance with these words I have made a covenant with you and with Israel.' Moses was there with the LORD forty days and forty nights without eating bread or drinking water. And he wrote on the tablets the words of the covenant—the Ten Commandments" (Exodus 34:27-28).*

Moses had just finished two back-to-back 40-day fasts. He had totally emptied himself so he could be totally filled with God. The words that God spoke to Moses in those quiet times together turned out to be some of the longest lasting words in the history of the world: the Ten Commandments. Three thousand years later they are still some of the most talked-about and cherished words ever written.

Our quiet times with God have power. This Exodus study is proof of that to me. It was during my own 40-day fast, almost three years before writing this devotional, that I first took the notes from the book of Exodus that have resulted in this study. What we do in our quiet times with God can have an effect days, months and even years into the future.

God wants us to spend time with Him, and to act on what He tells us to do during that time. God will do His part. He just wants us to do ours.

Lesson 45

Spending Time In God's Presence Changes Us

Scripture Reading: Exodus 34:29-35

If you've ever read through the book of Psalms, you may have noticed that King David doesn't always go into God's presence with a really happy attitude, but he usually comes out with one.

Just flip through the Psalms and see how many times this happens. Psalm 4, for instance, starts with, *"Answer me when I call to you, O my righteous God. Give me relief from my distress; be merciful to me and hear my prayer" (verse 1),* but it ends with, *"I will lie down in peace, for you alone, O LORD, make me dwell in safety" (verse 8).*

Over and over the pattern repeats. David starts out pretty angry with God, and angry with the people around him, but he ends up by praising God and trusting Him completely. Why?

Because spending time in God's presence changes us. Sometimes we don't even notice the change, but others do. And when they notice the change in us, it changes them, too.

Take a look at the change that took place in Moses when he spent time in God's presence. In Exodus chapter 34, the change was so visible, it was reflected in his face:

"When Moses came down from Mount Sinai with the two tablets of the Testimony in his hands, he was not aware that his face was radiant because he had spoken with the LORD. When Aaron and all the Israelites saw Moses, his face was radiant, and they were afraid to come near him. But Moses called to them; so Aaron and all the leaders of the community came back to him, and he spoke to them. Afterward all the Israelites came near him, and he gave them all the commands the LORD had given him on Mount Sinai. When Moses finished speaking to them, he put a veil over his face. But whenever he entered the LORD's presence to speak with him, he removed the veil until he came out. And when he came out and told the Israelites what he had been commanded, they saw that his face was radiant. Then Moses would put the veil back over his face until he went in to speak with the LORD" (Exodus 34:29-35).

Spending Time In God's Presence Changes Us

Here's a man with a super-tan! Moses had just asked God in Exodus chapter 33: "Show me your glory." Later, when Moses came down from the mountain, he had God's glory all over him! He was so radiant, so physically changed, that he had to put a veil over his face when he talked to other people!

Spending time in God's presence changes us. The more time we spend with God, the more we're changed we'll be—physically, emotionally, spiritually—in all kinds of ways. Whenever we ask to see God's glory, we shouldn't be surprised to find that His glory is reflected in us.

What causes the moon to shine so bright? It's the reflection of the sun. There's nothing inherent in the moon to make it light up the night. That's what God wants to do through each one of us. He wants us to spend time with Him, absorbing His glory, so we can go out and reflect the light of His Son into the darkness of the world around us.

Moses wasn't even aware how his time with God had changed him. But others were. The glory that covered Moses was certainly for Moses' benefit, but it also overflowed to all of those around him.

If you'll diligently spend time with God, you'll start to see that the overflow from your time with Him will naturally touch other people. Although this may not be your main purpose for spending time with God, He can use the overflow of your experience to "prime the pump" for others.

Spending time in God's presence changes us. Although you may come into His presence tired, angry, frustrated or broken, chances are good that a little time with the Creator of the universe, the One who gave you life and breath, will give you new life, too. He'll restore you, encourage you, strengthen you and help you to put your trust in Him more and more.

Lesson 46

MAKE THE CALL TO THE WILLING AND SKILLED

Scripture Reading: Exodus 35:1-36:7

If God has put a vision on your heart to do something for Him, I want to encourage you today to take a step of faith: make the call to all who are willing and skilled to help you do what God wants done.

If you're like me, asking for help is one of the hardest parts of carrying out God's will. But I'm encouraged by what I read in Exodus chapter 35. Here we see that Moses has come down from the mountain with a detailed vision in mind for what God wanted him to do next: to build an incredible place of worship for God. Now, it's time for Moses to ask the people for their help, to see if they will provide the resources and the labor to make it happen. How will he ask them? And how will they respond? Let's take a look:

"Moses said to the whole Israelite community, 'This is what the LORD has commanded: From

what you have, take an offering for the LORD. Everyone who is willing is to bring to the LORD an offering of gold, silver and bronze; blue, purple and scarlet yarn and fine linen; goat hair; ram skins dyed red and hides of sea cows; acacia wood; olive oil for the light; spices for the anointing oil and for the fragrant incense; and onyx stones and other gems to be mounted on the ephod and breastpiece. All who are skilled among you are to come and make everything the LORD has commanded...'" (Exodus 35:4-10).

He calls on all who are willing and skilled to "give" to the work and to "get involved" in the work. Now let's look at the response:

"Then the whole Israelite community withdrew from Moses' presence, and everyone who was willing and whose heart moved him came and brought an offering to the LORD for the work on the Tent of Meeting, for all its service, and for the sacred garments. ... All the Israelite men and women who were willing brought to the LORD freewill offerings for all the work the LORD through Moses had commanded them to do" (Exodus 35:21, 29).

In the end, God had stirred the hearts of

so many people that they had to be restrained from giving any more!

> *"Then Moses gave an order and they sent this word throughout the camp: 'No man or woman is to make anything else as an offering for the sanctuary.' And so the people were restrained from bringing more, because what they already had was more than enough to do all the work" (Exodus 36:6-7).*

When I first read this passage, I wondered what that must feel like, to see people give and get involved to such an extent that they had to be restrained from giving any more. But when I came back to this passage again to teach it to others, I was in the middle of raising funds for five of us to go on a missions trip to Africa. Up to that point, I had often questioned if we'd be able to raise enough for even one of us to go, let alone five.

I took encouragement from this passage, and kept pressing on. In the final weeks before our trip, I found myself having to tell people to not give any more to the trip, for we had already raised all that we needed for all five of us to go.

We can sometimes look at a passage like

this, and even hear a story like I just told, and be either discouraged or encouraged, wondering why it's not happening to us, or looking forward to when it will happen to us.

My encouragement to you is to make the call. Make the call to all who are willing to help you carry out the vision that God has put on your heart. As Christians, God has entrusted us with great visions, great plans and great ways to reach the world for Him. God wants us to step out in faith, make the call, and ask people to give and get involved in doing what God wants done. Make the call!

Lesson 47

Do
The Work

Scripture Reading: Exodus 36:8-39:32

I don't know about you, but there are times when I've planned, prayed and gotten things ready to take on a huge project, but by the time it comes to do the work, I'm already exhausted! I feel like a woman who's nine months pregnant, but when it comes time to push, I don't have the strength.

When we feel like we can't push any farther, that's often when we need to push the most. That's often the culmination of all that we've worked so hard to achieve up to that point. If we stop pushing at the moment of delivery, we're going to shortchange, and possibly even abort, the whole plan.

We've come to that point in the book of Exodus, too. We're on Lesson 47 out of 50. With just three lessons to go, the people are finally ready to do the work that God had given Moses such a detailed vision for back on the mountaintop. Take a look at just a few of the verses as the work begins:

> *"All the skilled men among the workmen made the tabernacle with ten curtains of finely twisted linen and blue, purple and scarlet yarn, with cherubim worked into them by a skilled craftsman. All the curtains were the same size—twenty-eight cubits long and four cubits wide. They joined five of the curtains together and did the same with the other five. Then they made loops of blue material along the edge of the end curtain in one set, and the same was done with the end curtain in the other set. They also made fifty loops on one curtain and fifty loops on the end curtain of the other set, with the loops opposite each other. Then they made fifty gold clasps and used them to fasten the two sets of curtains together so that the tabernacle was a unit"* (Exodus 36:8-13).

The description of all the work continues in similar detail for another three chapters. Sometimes we can skip over these details in the Bible, but this is the foundation for what God called them to do. They came out of the desert to worship God, and now they're building a place of worship to do it.

When I studied this passage initially, I heard about a songwriting contest. I had written a song about five years earlier that I really liked and had put a lot of time into, but never recorded it. The contest turned out to be just the thing I needed to finally spur me on to do the work and get it recorded. Although I didn't exactly have the time to mess with this kind of thing, I felt like I needed to follow through on all the work I had previously done on the song.

So I stepped out of my comfort zone and sent an email to a woman in California. I loved her voice, but didn't have any money to pay her for this project. I asked her if she'd still be willing to record the song for this contest, anyway. Amazingly, she said, "Yes," and asked some of her friends to help her record it.

It turned out to be a beautiful recording, and although we didn't win the contest, I was so thankful to have it recorded. When I called to thank her for her work on it, she said, "Oh, no, thank you! Thank you for asking and letting me do it!" She told me how the song had really ministered to her that week as she worked on it. Had I not "made the call" to get the work done, the song still wouldn't be recorded, and those involved would have missed out on the blessing it turned out to be to them as well.

I know how hard it can be to "do the work" when the time finally comes to do it.

But for whatever project God's given you, don't lose heart. Don't lose strength. This final push could be what finally delivers your "baby." Many people will be blessed through your work, including those who work on it with you!

So don't give up. Don't give in. Don't stop pushing now. Do the work! And get it done!

Lesson 48

Finish The Work

Scripture Reading: Exodus 39:33-40:33

We're just around the corner from the end of this study of the book of Exodus. Appropriately, then, this lesson is called, "Finish The Work."

Today is "payday" for Moses and for all the people traveling with him. They're about to reach the culmination of all that they've worked for, and all that they've been set free for: to worship God.

The details of their work, as listed in Exodus chapters 39 and 40, might seem trivial, dull and something to skip over to someone just skimming through the Bible. But if you've ever worked on a building project yourself, you know that when the end of the project starts coming into view, those days can be some of the most exciting and beautiful days of the entire project!

Can you imagine what the people who were building this place of worship must have thought as they saw it all finally coming together? They've just carved all these beautiful things, gilded them with gold, and decorated them with all kinds of precious stones. They've just crafted beautiful works of art that were conceived in the very mind of God Himself.

Then they started bringing them forward to Moses, letting him look over each item to see that it was finished exactly as God had described them to him on the mountain. They begin to put it all together, standing each piece up in its place. They light the lamps, burn the incense, and put the tablets of stone, the very words of God, into the ark of the covenant, and Wow! The work is finally complete!

The whole process concludes with these words:

"So all the work on the tabernacle, the Tent of Meeting, was completed. The Israelites did everything just as the LORD commanded Moses....And so Moses finished the work" (Exodus 39:32, 40:33b).

What a powerful moment! Have you ever

heard about something called the "212 Principle," popularized in a book by Mac Anderson and Sam Parker? At 211 degrees Fahrenheit, water is hot, but at 212 degrees, water boils. And when water boils, you get steam, and steam can power a locomotive. Although there's only one degree of difference between 211 and 212, that extra degree can be enough to take all the previous effort over the top!

I don't know what kind of project you might be working on right now. I don't know if you're at 211 degrees, or 150, or 98.6! But I do know that we all have a tendency to wear out when we're working on a project, even a project that God has clearly called us to do. We can get to the point where we're not sure if we can take one more step. We're not sure that we can raise the temperature one more degree. But let me encourage you that if God's called you to do it, keep on doing it!

The American inventor, Thomas Edison, worked non-stop for several years to perfect the light bulb. He tested over 6,000 materials to use for filaments—everything from bamboo to cedar to hickory. After thousands of tests and a pile of failed materials that stacked up outside his house high enough to reach his second floor window, Edison finally hit upon a material that burned long enough, and bright enough, for commercial success: carbonized cotton.

Edison's perseverance paid off, not only for himself, but for all of us who have benefited from his perseverance. Edison said, "Many of life's failures were men who did not realize how close they were to success when they gave up."

The Apostle Paul, who knew how hard it was to persevere in the work of the Lord year after year, even in the face of endless persecution, hardship and personal suffering, still had enough confidence in the end result of that perseverance that he wrote to the people living in Galatia: *"Let us not become weary in doing good, for at the proper time we will reap a harvest if we do not give up"* (Galatians 6:9).

Don't become weary in doing good! Finish the work! At the proper time, you will reap a harvest, if you do not give up.

Lesson 49

THE GLORY OF THE LORD COVERS THE WORK

Scripture Reading: Exodus 40:34-38

We've come to the last five verses, and the spectacular conclusion, of the book of Exodus. Take a look at what happens when Moses finishes the work:

> *"Then the cloud covered the Tent of Meeting, and the glory of the LORD filled the tabernacle. Moses could not enter the Tent of Meeting because the cloud had settled upon it, and the glory of the LORD filled the tabernacle. In all the travels of the Israelites, whenever the cloud lifted from above the tabernacle, they would set out; but if the cloud did not lift, they did not set out—until the day it lifted. So the cloud of the LORD was over the tabernacle by day, and fire was in the cloud by night, in the sight of all the house of Israel during all their travels" (Exodus 40:34-38).*

What is it that Moses sees that so fills the

tabernacle that he can't even get into it? The glory of the Lord—the very thing that Moses had asked to see back in Exodus 33:18 when he said, "Now show me your glory." But this time, Moses wasn't the only one who got to see it—everyone got to see it!

There's a lesson here for me, for you and for everyone who does their work as if working for the Lord: when you've finished the work, been obedient to the vision, and brought it to its conclusion, the glory of the Lord can finally come down on your work in a way that everyone can see it.

I've had some experiences in my life where I've sensed the presence of God in a way that I can only describe as "the glory of the Lord." I'm not an expert in the glory of the Lord, but from what I've read in the Bible, from what I've learned from other Christians, and from what I've experienced in my own life, the glory of the Lord seems to be actual "stuff," like the air we breathe. It's real, physical and tangible. It can be seen, sensed and felt.

I've sensed it during worship, when one time I was just singing to God in what seemed to be a normal, enjoyable worship experience, and all of a sudden, the presence of the Lord was so real and tangible that I felt like I couldn't move if I wanted to. And I didn't want to! I wanted to stay in His presence as long as I possibly could!

I've sensed it during my quiet times, when once I was sitting back on my couch, writing in my journal, and suddenly felt like melted butter was being poured into my chest. Maybe it was the oil of the Holy Spirit, if that sounds more palatable, but whatever words I would use to describe it couldn't do justice to what I felt during those precious minutes with the Lord.

I'd love to be able to finish a project and see the glory of the Lord come down and cover it in a way that everyone could see it, so that I couldn't even stand up anymore! At that point, I wouldn't care! If my purpose in doing all that I do is to worship the Lord, as was the case for the Israelites, then who cares if He bowls me over when it's done, and I'm laid out flat on the floor in His presence? That's right where I'd want to be anyway! I wouldn't want to go anywhere else!

If the Lord picked up and moved, I'd want to pick up and move with Him, like the Israelites who followed Him. I wouldn't want to stay back! I'd want to be with God!

My prayer for you as you work on your own projects for the Lord, and even as you come to the the end of this study with me, is that when you've finished the work, been obedient to the vision, and brought it to its conclusion, that the glory of the Lord would show up in such a way that you, and everyone else, can see it.

Now, may the Lord show you His glory!

Lesson 50

FREE TO WORSHIP

Scripture Reading: Exodus 3:12

Thanks for taking the time to go through this study of the book of Exodus with me. I've learned a lot from the story of how God set the Israelites free, and I hope you have, too.

As we close out our time together, I'd like to remind you of three key points from this study that apply directly to each of our lives.

1) God set the Israelites free so they could worship Him—and that's the same reason He set you free, too.

This reason is stated throughout the book of Exodus, from the first time that God called to Moses from the burning bush: *"When you have brought the people out of Egypt, you will worship God on this mountain' " (Exodus 3:12b).*

To the words Moses spoke to Pharaoh: *"Go to Pharaoh and say to him, 'This is what the*

LORD *says: Let my people go, so that they may worship me' " (Exodus 8:1b).*

To the concluding scene of the entire book, when the glory of the Lord descended on the place the Israelites built to worship Him: *"Then the cloud covered the Tent of Meeting, and the glory of the LORD filled the tabernacle" (Exodus 40:34).*

To be truly free means to be able to worship God with your whole heart. If you can worship God with your whole heart, regardless of whatever else might be going on around you, you're free! But if you can't worship God in your heart, for whatever reason, you're still in bondage, and God wants to set you free.

If that's the case, you might want to review these lessons again to look for ideas to help you get fully free.

2) God helped the Israelites to stay free—and He wants to help you stay free, too.

God's help included a system of rules to keep the Israelites, and each of us, from plunging back into bondage again. These rules are summarized in the Ten Commandments:

> *"You shall have no other gods before me...*
> *You shall not make for yourself an idol...*
> *You shall not misuse the name of the LORD your God...*
> *Remember the Sabbath day by keeping it holy...*
> *Honor your father and your mother...*
> *You shall not murder.*
> *You shall not commit adultery.*
> *You shall not steal.*
> *You shall not give false testimony against your neighbor.*
> *You shall not covet..." (from Exodus 20:1-17).*

Rather than restricting us, these rules free us to live the abundant life God has created us to live.

Again, if you've gotten free in the past, but are struggling to stay free now, you might want to review these lessons again for more insights on how to restore the freedom you once had.

3) God invited Moses to take part in His plan to set

others free—just like God is inviting you to take part in it, too.

Hundreds of years before Moses was even born, God had a plan for setting the Israelites free. God told Abraham:

"Know for certain that your descendants will be strangers in a country not their own, and they will be enslaved and mistreated four hundred years. But I will punish the nation they serve as slaves, and afterward they will come out with great possessions" (Genesis 15:14).

And that's exactly what happened. God had a plan in mind for setting His people free, and He called on Moses to help Him with that plan.

God has a plan for setting others free, too, and He's called on you and me to help Him with that plan.

What's His plan? God knew that our sins would enslave us—and eventually kill us. So God sent Jesus, His Son, to die for our sins so we could be free to live with Him forever:

"For God so loved the world that he gave his one

and only Son, that whoever believes in him shall not perish but have eternal life" (John 3:16).

After dying for our freedom, and rising again from the dead, Jesus asked His followers to do one more thing:

"Go into all the world and preach the good news to all creation" (Mark 16:15).

He's inviting you into His plan. Won't you join Him?

About The Author

Described by *USA Today* as "a new breed of evangelist," Eric Elder is an ordained pastor, songwriter and the creator of *The Ranch,* a faith-boosting website that attracts thousands of visitors each month at WWW.THERANCH.ORG.

Eric is also an inspirational writer and speaker, having written about spiritual issues for publications like Billy Graham's *Decision Magazine,* and spoken about freedom at national conferences like the *Exodus International Freedom Conference.*

This fresh work, filled with personal stories and practical applications, brings to life stories from the Bible that have been inspiring people for over 3,000 years.

To listen to, download or order more inspiring resources, please visit:

WWW.THE RANCH.ORG

Made in the USA